CLASSROOM BEHAVIOR
Detecting and Correcting Special Problems

Joyce S. Choate/*Consulting Editor*

FRANK J. SPARZO
Ball State University

JAMES A. POTEET
Ball State University

ALLYN AND BACON
Boston / London / Sydney / Toronto

THE ALLYN AND BACON DETECTING AND CORRECTING SERIES

Joyce S. Choate, *Consulting Editor*

A Division of Simon & Schuster
160 Gould Street
Needham Heights, MA 02194-2310

Portions of Part I are adapted from F. J. Sparzo, *Changing Behavior: A Practical Guide for Teachers and Parents* (Bloomington, IN: Phi Delta Kappa Educational Foundation, 1985). Used with permission.

Editorial-Production Service: Karen G. Mason
Copyeditor: Susan Freese
Cover Administrator: Linda K. Dickinson
Cover Designer: Susan Slovinsky

Library of Congress Cataloging-in-Publication Data

Sparzo, Frank J.
Classroom behavior, detecting and correcting special needs / authors, Frank J. Sparzo, James A. Poteet
p. cm. — (The Allyn and Bacon detecting and correcting series)
Includes index.
ISBN 0-205-11634-5
1. Classroom management — United States. 2. School children — United States — Discipline. 3. Problem children—Education—United States. I. Poteet, James A. II. Title. III. Series.
LB3013.S635 1988
371.1'024—dc19 88-10180
CIP

Printed in the United States of America

10 9 8 7 6 5 4 3 2 93 92

Contents

LIST OF TABLES AND FIGURES

Foreword

ABOUT THE *DETECTING AND CORRECTING SERIES*

Classroom Behavior: Detecting and Correcting Special Problems is one of several books in an affordable series that focuses on the classroom needs of special students, both exceptional and nonexceptional, who often require adjusted methods and curricula. The purpose of this book, as well as the others, is to supplement more comprehensive and theoretical treatments of major instructional issues—in this case, solving behavior problems—with practical classroom practices.

The underlying theme of each book in the *Allyn and Bacon Detecting and Correcting Series* is targeted instruction to maximize students' progress in school. Designed for informed teachers and teachers-in-training who are responsible for instructing special students in a variety of settings, these books emphasize the application of theory to everyday classroom concerns. While this approach may not be unique, the format in which both theme and purpose are presented is, in that it enables the reader to quickly translate theory into practical classroom strategies for reaching hard-to-reach students.

Each book begins with an overview of general principles and procedures, addressing in particular the needs of special students. The groundwork is laid here for both Detection and Correction—observing students' difficulties and then designing an individualized prescriptive program. Remaining chapters are organized into sequentially numbered units, addressing specific problems of special students. Each unit follows a consistent two-part format. Detection is addressed first, beginning with a citation of a few significant behaviors and continuing with a discussion of factors such as descriptions and implications. The second part of each unit is Correction, where a number of principles or strategies are offered for modification according to students' learning needs.

This simple, consistent format makes the *Detecting and Correcting* books accessible and easy to read. Other useful features include: a) the Contents organization designed for quick location of problem skills and behaviors; b) cross-references among units; c) a "Reflections" section ending each part, providing discussion and application activities; and d) an index of general topics and cross-references to related subjects.

Along with the topics of related books—reading, language arts, and basic mathematics—classroom behavior represents a major area in which special students often require special accommodations. Together, these books comprise the first installment of what is envisioned to be a larger series that simplifies teachers' tasks by offering sound and practical classroom procedures for detecting and correcting special needs and problems.

Joyce S. Choate
Consulting Editor

Preface

Every teacher knows students who need special help to meet the social and academic demands of the classroom. Some students engage in excessive behaviors such as hitting or swearing, while others exhibit deficiencies such as inattention or unsatisfactory homework. Still other students respond inappropriately to a variety of classroom cues exemplified by being tardy or breaking rules.

Many problems involving excessive, deficit, or inappropriate behavior are due not so much to psychological characteristics or inner states as to prior and current learning experiences. Consider, for example, Todd, a student who puts things off. He delays doing his homework until near bedtime, falls days behind on his chores, and turns in most school assignments late, if at all. It is appropriate to summarize these delay tactics by saying that Todd procrastinates. But it is at best misleading to explain Todd's delays by saying that he puts things off *because* he is a procrastinator (or lazy, or unmotivated).

Though explanations of this sort are commonplace, they tend to stop inquiry into the actual reasons for behavior, in this case, procrastination. Rather than invoke psychological labels to explain behavior, the approach presented in these pages focuses on past and current conditions that underlie problem behaviors. In the case of procrastination, for example, we may well discover that putting things off leads to a variety of immediate payoffs that outweigh possible future problems that accompany procrastination.

ASSUMPTIONS

The principles and procedures discussed in these pages are derived from the field of behavior analysis. Since the study of human behavior is still largely a matter of interpretation and is likely to remain so for many years to come, no claim is made that the interventions listed for each behavior problem have been tested and found to work for that problem. Nor is *Classroom Behavior: Detecting and Correcting Special Problems* a substitute for thorough study and supervised clinical work in applied behavior analysis; there is no substitute for such an education. But this does not mean that the deliberate use of behavioral principles is off limits to teachers with less than full knowledge of the field. On the contrary, the following assumptions have guided this work:

1. Most classsroom behavior problems are largely a function of the environmental conditions under which they occur.

2. Teachers who are knowledgeable in basic principles of behavior can systematically change social and academic behaviors which interfere with teaching and learning.
3. Classroom behavior problems are similar across several categories of students, including students described as regular, remedial, gifted and talented, culturally different, and handicapped.
4. Severe and long standing behavior problems require the assistance of specially trained professionals.

This book is intended for use as a field resource and supplementary text by teachers and prospective teachers who are concerned with solving behavior problems in the classroom. A *practical* complement to theoretical texts and teaching wisdom, it is deliberately brief and concise. The intent is to enable the reader to translate principles of behavior change into practical classroom strategies to improve the social and academic performance of students. Whether your interest is teaching regular, remedial, or special education students, you will find the information in *Classroom Behavior: Detecting and Correcting Special Problems* quite relevant to your daily concerns.

ORGANIZATION

The book is divided into two major parts. Each part begins with an overview and concludes with suggestions for reflecting on its content. "Reflections" are intended for reader clarification, discussion, interpretation, and application. The final item in "Reflections" is a listing of additional resources for further information. The table of contents is designed to provide an at-a-glance guide for locating specific behavior problems.

Part I of the book presents general concepts for changing behavior and also outlines a basic plan for increasing and reducing behavior. Chapter 1 introduces the basic plan, consisting of nine steps:

1. Define behavior
2. Observe and record behavior
3. Set attainable goals
4. Identify potential rewards
5. Select procedures
6. Rehearse procedures
7. Implement plan
8. Monitor results
9. Maintain gains

The remaining four chapters in Part I elaborate on each of the nine steps of the general plan.

Part II contains suggestions for responding to behavior problems that teachers face almost daily. Utilizing a problem-oriented format, behaviors are grouped into eight categories that incorporate problems related to performing school and academic tasks, verbal behavior, aggression, dishonesty, social interaction, immaturity, sense of self, and body and personal habits. Each of the first 34 problems is discussed in terms of its description, its implications, and its controlling factors. A number of corrective procedures are then suggested for each problem, usually listed from least to most intrusive. Part II concludes with a brief discussion of special populations. Problems 35 and 36 are cross-referenced with preceding discussions and focus on several behaviors that may be exhibited by special populations, both nonhandicapped and handicapped.

The 36 behavior problems are among the ones frequently cited by teachers as troublesome. When these problems are not severe and longstanding, they can be handled, in most cases, by the skillful application of the principles and procedures described in this book.

HOW TO USE THIS BOOK

This book should be especially useful when problems in performance resist routine attempts to solve them. When this happens, we suggest this sequence: 1) Become thoroughly familiar with the general principles and procedures presented in Part I; 2) read about the specific problem that concerns you in Part II; and 3) incorporate what you have learned into the basic nine-step plan for changing behavior described in Chapter 1. *You should also consult additional references and appropriate professionals whenever you find they are needed.* A number of references are included in the book for this purpose.

ACKNOWLEDGMENTS

The authors wish to acknowledge the assistance of Joyce Choate who was instrumental from the inception of the book to its final copy. The book was strengthened by the comments and suggestions of William H. Evans, University of West Florida and Gail McGee, University of Massachusetts. And a special thanks goes to Mylan Jaixen at Allyn and Bacon for his exceptionally patient behavior.

PART I

GENERAL CONCEPTS AND PRINCIPLES

Part I of this book presents a general plan for increasing and reducing social and academic behaviors. The general plan is appropriate when we want to alter behavior in some deliberate and systematic way.

Although the plan is presented in nine steps, there is nothing sacred about the number of steps. Sometimes, for example, the plan can be easily implemented by simply specifying a behavior (step 1), applying a strategy (step 7), and noting the result (step 8). On other occasions, most or all of the steps in the plan are necessary to alter student performance. Sometimes, too, the entire plan can be put into effect quite easily (in a matter of minutes), as in the case of the elementary school teacher described in Chapter 1. On other occasions, as in the case of the ninth-grade teacher described in Chapter 4, the plan may extend over several weeks.

It is important that you apply the principles and procedures presented in Part I more like an artist than a mechanic. There are no hard-and-fast rules, no "cookbook" methods to be applied without careful analysis. Remember that all students are unique. Thus, what is effective with one student may be ineffective with another. This is nowhere more apparent than in the area of motivation. Some students relish teacher praise, while others prefer athletics and peer approval to most forms of teacher attention. And some students will stop swearing when you ask them to stop, while others will stop only in response to losing some privilege.

It is also important to pay special attention to the principles in Chapter 4 for selecting and using reinforcers (see "Some Preliminary Concerns") before applying any of the change strategies presented in this book.

Part I consists of five chapters. Chapter 1 presents fundamental principles and procedures for altering behavior. The major message of the chapter is that teachers are likely to be in a good position to change behavior if they pay close attention to what students do and the conditions under which they do it. The chapter also introduces a nine-step plan for behavior change. You are thereby advised to give careful attention to the contents of Chapter 1. You are also advised to take the Self-Quiz at the end of this chapter and subsequent chapters in Part I.

After specifying three criteria for defining behavior (step 1), Chapter 2 outlines some of the ways to observe student behavior directly (step 2). The chapter includes several observational techniques not normally used by teachers. You will learn about the importance of setting attainable goals (step 3) and identifying potential motivators (step 4) in Chapter 3. No step in the general plan is more important than this one. You should consult Chapter 4 often. It provides brief descriptions of strategies for increasing and reducing student behavior (step 5).

The order in which the reductive strategies are listed in Chapter 4 is important for ethical reasons. A clear preference is shown for instruction, situational changes, and reinforcement procedures over aversive techniques. Hopefully, this preference will influence teachers to employ the most humane procedures possible in their attempts to discipline students.

The final chapter in Part I, Chapter 5, presents a brief overview of steps 6 (rehearsal), 7 (implementation), 8 (monitoring), and 9 (maintaining gains) in the general behavior change plan. Whether you teach students in regular education, remedial education, or special education, you will find the principles and procedures in Part I quite relevant to your daily concerns.

Classroom learning may be defined as a change in student behavior resulting from conditions arranged by a teacher. Most people would agree that learning, viewed as behavior change that generalizes outside the school setting, is the major goal of all classroom teaching. In this chapter, we will discuss a behavior change methodology derived from the field of behavior analysis and outlined by Sparzo (1985).

Whenever we want to change student behavior in some deliberate and systematic way, it is important to focus on the relationship between the behavior we want to change and the events that come before and after it. Events that come before behavior are termed *antecedent* or A events, while those that follow are termed *consequent* or C events. We will use the letter B to refer to the behavior (intellectual, motor, emotional, social) that concerns us.

If, for example, you present a problem to a student, the problem is an A event, the student's response to the problem is a B event, and the feedback that follows the behavior is a C event. This ABC analysis is applied to the teaching episodes below. Note that the ABC analysis is applied to a wide range of behaviors, which may be classified under the headings of academic behavior, classroom management, athletics, or even aspects of emotion.

We start with academic behavior. Mr. Jones asked his students to determine the cost of the bottle when a bottle of liquid costs $10.00, and the liquid alone costs $9.00 more than the bottle. Some students immediately said that the bottle cost $1.00. Mr. Jones said, "Remember that the liquid costs $9.00 more than the bottle. Nine dollars minus $1.00 means that the bottle costs only $8.00 more than the liquid." After several additional attempts, Mr. Jones provided an additional clue: "Try thinking algebraically." A student immediately said, "The bottle costs $.50." "Right!" said Mr. Jones.

Mary could not spell *asphyxiate.* After writing *asphyxiate* on the chalkboard, her teacher asked Mary to spell the word aloud five times, use it in a sentence, then write the word. Her efforts were praised by the teacher.

An ABC analysis can be applied to the situations above. Mr. Jones's presentation of the math problem and his clues are antecedent (A) events, the students' attempts to solve the problem are behavioral (B) events, and the corrective feedback from Mr. Jones is a consequent (C) event. The analysis is similar for Mary. Writing *asphyxiate* on the chalkboard and giving directions are antecedent (A) events, while Mary's responses are behavioral (B) events. Teacher praise is an obvious consequent (C) event.

Although we are being quite general in our analysis, it can be seen that an ABC analysis is appropriate not only for behaviors that relate to academic work but, as sketched below, to classroom management, to athletic skills, and to aspects of emotion as well.

In a situation concerning classroom management, the teacher noted that Jimmy left his seat without permission several times a day. This behavior was interfering with his academic progress. After the rule for staying seated was explained to him, Jimmy was given access to special privileges every time he remained seated for a prespecified period of time. Over a period of several weeks, Jimmy learned to leave his seat only with permission.

Joan hit her classmates from time to time. After clarifying the various ways in which Joan hit others, Ms. Elliot, Joan's teacher, implemented the following plan: Joan would owe time (five minutes) each time she hit someone. Owed time would be paid back after school. Joan's rate of hitting slowly declined.

An ABC analysis can be applied to athletic settings. For example, because Coach Lane's basketball team was shooting a paltry 28% at the free-throw line, he required each player to shoot one hundred additional free throws during each practice session. The team's free-throw percentage gradually rose to 56%.

The analysis can also be useful in looking at emotional reactions. For example, Tim returned to school after the death of his mother. Tim's teacher, Mr. Church, discussed Tim's loss with the students prior to Tim's return. The discussion included suggestions for responding to Tim in an effort to make him feel more comfortable. The implemented suggestions did seem to increase Tim's sense of security.

With respect to out-of-seat behavior, reviewing the rule for sitting was an important A event, Jimmy's response to the rule was a B event, and receiving special privileges were C events. Joan's hitting behavior can also be viewed in terms of an ABC analysis. The demonstration was an A event, hitting was a B event, and owing five minutes each time hitting occurred was a C event. Coach Lane's practice requirement was an A event, the practice itself involved B events, and signs of progress, C events. Finally, Mr. Church's suggestions were A events, their applications were B events, and signs that Tim felt more comfortable, C events.

MORE ABOUT ANTECEDENTS

Why does a student answer a question when asked? Or why does a student go to recess at the appropriate time? The answers lie in the student's past learning experiences. People learn to respond to environmental cues because they have been reinforced (rewarded) for doing so.

The process by which an individual learns to respond to the right antecedent stimuli or events but not to the wrong ones is termed *discrimination learning*. Essentially, this procedure involves rewarding an action when a particular stimulus or event is present and not rewarding it when other stimuli or events are present. Thus, only a certain stimulus or event comes to cue the action. Most of the time, several antecedent events control an individual's actions, as they do, for example, when a person enters an elevator after the "up" light comes on, the doors open, a tone sounds, and the individual observes others moving in the direction of the elevator.

What has been described is not unlike what occurs when, for example, a person does one thing in one situation but says the opposite in another. Acting with duplicity is sometimes called *hypocrisy*. But what has actually happened? The person has learned to discriminate between the situations. In the first situation, he has probably been rewarded for acting in a certain way; in the other setting, talking in a contrary way has brought rewards. Note that here the explanation for hypocrisy is found mainly in environmental circumstances, not within the person in the form of a characteristic or trait called hypocrisy.

The relationship between an ABC analysis and such complex topics as instruction, modeling, and behavior governed by rules is represented in Table 1-1 on the next page.

MORE ABOUT CONSEQUENCES

Most of the time, what comes after an act is as important as what comes before it. People are often unaware of how much they are affected by the events that follow their actions. Some teachers, for example, are unaware that attending to misbehavior after it occurs may actually increase it. This section takes a look at consequences (C), which include procedures called *reinforcement*, *extinction*, and *punishment*.

There are two types of reinforcers (rewards), positive and negative. Both maintain or increase behavior, but they do so in different ways. If something is added (presented) after a behavior and the behavior increases (for example, it increases in frequency, duration, force, or likelihood), the event is called a *positive reinforcer*. If something is subtracted (removed) or prevented after a response and behavior increases (for example, in frequency, duration, force, or likelihood), the event is termed a *negative reinforcer*.

Consider two cases: (1) Someone does a good deed because in the past good deeds have been followed by various forms of appreciation from others, and (2) a student completes most of his spelling assignment early in exchange for time on a computer. Both cases fit the definition of a positive

TABLE 1-1 An ABC Analysis and Complex Events

	Antecedent Event	Behavior	Consequent Event
Instruction (Verbal)	• Teacher asks a question	• Student answers the question	• Teacher says "Good"
	• Text presents a physics problem	• Student solves the problem	• Student earns an A grade
	• Teacher prompts: "It says meow."	• Child says: "Kitty."	• Teacher says: "Right!"
Modeling (Nonverbal)	• Coach demonstrates proper form	• Student imitates correctly	• Student shows good form
	• Student wears a new hairstyle	• Another student cuts hair to match	• Student gets attention
Rules	• Sign in pool area: "No Running"	• Students obey sign	• Students avoid punishment
	• Directions for lab experiment	• Students follow directions carefully	• Experiment is successful

reinforcer: Something was added or presented *and* behavior was maintained or increased. In the first case, appreciation was added and good deeds were likely to occur again. In the second case, time on the computer was added, making early completion of assignments likely. Good use of positive reinforcement is at the heart of effective instruction and classroom management.

Negative reinforcement may be illustrated (1) by a student who repeatedly hands over his lunch money when threatened by a bully and (2) by a student who scampers to his seat each time he hears his teacher approaching the classroom. In the first case, threats were removed by surrendering money. Thus, a behavior (surrendering money) was strengthened by the subtraction of something (threats). In the second case, rushing to one's seat is also negatively reinforced because it prevents a possible aversive reaction by the teacher for being out-of-seat.

Try applying these definitions to the following situations.

SITUATION	WRITE YOUR ANSWER HERE
1. Sally always kept a neat desk and thereby avoided her teacher's reprimands.	______________
2. Dick got a smile from his teacher when he turned in his assignment.	______________
3. Ms. Taylor increased creative thinking by praising innovative rather than common responses.	______________

Since Sally prevented reprimands by keeping her desk neat and clean, her desk-clearing behavior was negatively rewarded. In Dick's case, since no change in behavior was specified or implied, no interpretation about the effect of the teacher's smile on Dick's future behavior can be made. It is important to remember that a reinforcer is defined by its effect on behavior, not by whether something looks like a reinforcing event. And Ms. Taylor increased creativity by providing positive reinforcement (praise) for innovative responses.

Hidden Influences

We sometimes see students do things for which they get no reward. But what we see may be more apparent than real. The next time you think you are observing such a situation, consider three very important points:

1. The student may be engaging in avoidance or escape behavior (i.e., negatively reinforced behavior) as we saw in the example above with Sally.
2. You may not be aware of the events in the student's life that are functioning as rewards. This point relates to the topic of classifying rewards, to be discussed later.
3. The behavior you are observing may be rewarded only occasionally and you are unaware of those occasions. This point relates to the topic of schedules of reinforcement, to be discussed later.

The concept of negative reinforcement helps us understand how people learn to avoid and escape many unpleasant things in life. Avoidance behavior, as in the Sally episode above, refers to behavior that prevents the possibility of unpleasant consequences; escape behavior refers to behavior that terminates an existing unpleasant consequence. Technically, Sally did not escape from her teacher's reprimands since they were threatened but not delivered. Lying, sneaking, cheating, and truancy are essentially negatively reinforced behaviors because they enable people to avoid or escape from various punishing events.

Classifying Rewards. Rewards (and punishers) may be conveniently classified in four broad categories, although the categories overlap somewhat. Since everyone has unique genetic and environmental histories, what is rewarding and punishing varies considerably, of course, from one person to another. A few reinforcers are listed in Table 1-2.

TABLE 1-2 Categories of Reinforcers

Social Rewards	Activity Rewards	Tangible Rewards	Primary Rewards
Attention	Reading	Money	Air
Touching	Free time	Coupons	Food
Praise	Thinking	Grades	Water
Smiles	Watching TV	Books	Sleep
Proximity	Running errands	Jewelry	Sex

This classification scheme has considerable practical value. It calls attention to the enormous range and variety of events that can serve as consequences for our actions, although the lists provide only a slight hint of that range and variety. It is important to point out that what a person finds rewarding can be quite individualistic. Some students respond very positively to a kind word or praise (social rewards), some relish free time (activity reward), others will do almost anything for access to the family car (tangible and activity rewards), while others especially like sleeping in (primary reward).

Moreover, reinforcers can be almost any event, not just those controlled by the teacher. For example, the laughter of other students, seeing the teacher upset, a dropped book, and being sent to the principal's office can all function as reinforcement for various behaviors.

Reinforcement Schedules. When behavior is rewarded each time it occurs, it is said to be on a continuous schedule of reward. When machines (e.g., automobiles, elevators, electric toasters, TV sets) are kept in good working order, they reward behavior continuously. For example, people are rewarded by the sound and picture each time they turn on their television set. Continuous schedules of reinforcement are advantageous when new behaviors are being taught. Once a behavior is established, however, it is generally best to switch to an intermittent or partial schedule of reinforcement. (We do, of course, want our mechanical devices to reward us continuously.)

Behavior that is rewarded only occasionally is on an intermittent schedule of reward. These intermittent schedules occur in a wide variety of ways and are especially prevalent in social situations. Raised hands in anticipation of teacher's attention, shooting baskets on the basketball court, and responding to examination questions are nearly always rewarded on intermittent schedules.

How often behavior is rewarded (i.e., its schedule of reward) has powerful and pervasive effects on behavior, although, as suggested earlier, the influence of schedules usually goes unnoticed. Each type of schedule has characteristic effects on behavior so long as the schedule remains constant. For example, when you want to maintain student behavior over a long period of time, make sure you reward it only occasionally, not continuously. Behavior is more likely to persist after reinforcement on an intermittent schedule than on a continuous schedule.

Behaviors that are commonly attributed to factors such as needs, drives, attitudes, and self-concept can often be more profitably attributed to the effects of schedules of reward. For instance, it you see a student working long and hard on a class or extracurricular project, he may be doing so not so much because of an inner need or drive or attitude or positive self-concept, but, apart from the intrinsic motivational properties of the project itself, because some reinforcement schedules generate high and stable rates of performance.

Discontinuation of Reinforcement (Extinction)

When a reward that has maintained a particular behavior is withheld or discontinued, the behavior is likely to weaken or decline in frequency. The term *extinction* is used to refer to this process. For example, if a teacher who has given attention to a student's tattling now ignores all instances of tattling (withholds the attention given previously), tattling will probably be reduced, at least in the presence of the teacher. Note that extinction, when it involves attention, is not synonymous with simply ignoring a behavior, because extinction involves withholding attention *previously given* to a behavior.

Social events are not the only events that can be involved in an extinction procedure. For instance, if a computer fails to work despite efforts to repair it, one quickly learns to stop using it.

Punishment

Punishment is another procedure used to reduce or eliminate a response. Because it can cause detrimental side effects, it should be used sparingly and with caution. For example, although punishment might eliminate a particular behavior, it could well elicit negative emotional reactions that linger far beyond the punishing incident itself.

There are two types of punishment, Type 1 (positive punishment) and Type 2 (negative punishment). If an event is added (presented) after a behavior occurs and the behavior is reduced (for example, the behavior decreases in frequency, duration, force, or likelihood), the event is a Type 1 punisher (positive punisher). If an event is subtracted or removed after a behavior occurs and the behavior is reduced, the event is a Type 2 punisher (negative punisher). Both procedures reduce or eliminate behavior. Reprimanding a student for an action is an example of Type 1 punishment, if the action weakens (an event is added and behavior is reduced). And taking away recess time contingent on misbehavior is an instance of Type 2 punishment, if misbehavior diminishes (something is subtracted and behavior is reduced).

Determine whether the following episodes illustrate extinction or punishment (Type 1 or Type 2).

EPISODE	WRITE YOUR ANSWER HERE
1. Peter's attempts to get a date with Jane were met with sarcasm. He no longer asks her out.	____________________
2. Gregory lost two minutes of free time for each minute he arrived late for class. He stopped coming late after his teacher applied the procedure several times.	____________________
3. Melissa started ignoring her classmate's complaints. Her classmate complains much less often now.	____________________

(1) Type 1 punishment (positive punishment) was applied to Peter's attempts to get a date with Jane; an aversive event was added and requests for dates stopped. (2) On the other hand, Gregory's behavior was weakened through a Type 2 punishment procedure (negative punishment) since a rewarding event (free time) was subtracted depending on his lateness. (3) Since Melissa withheld reinforcement (attention) and complaining decreased, this episode illustrates extinction.

NINE STEPS TO BEHAVIOR CHANGE

This chapter concludes by presenting a nine-step plan for changing behavior (Sparzo, 1985). Sometimes the plan will be implemented rather easily, sometimes not. The nine steps to behavior change are:

1. Define behavior
2. Observe and record behavior
3. Set attainable goals
4. Identify potential rewards
5. Select procedures
6. Rehearse procedures
7. Implement plan
8. Monitor results
9. Maintain gains

This plan is appropriate not only for changing someone else's behavior but also for changing one's own. It can be applied whenever there is too much behavior (an excess), too little behavior (a deficit), or inappropriate behavior. Verbal abuse and monopolizing conversations are usually behavioral excesses; poor academic performance and severe social withdrawal are examples of deficits. Breaches in etiquette are considered inappropriate behaviors in most situations. What is too much, too little, or inappropriate behavior requires a judgment call on your part. Falling behind in one's studies, for example, is not necessarily a problem in and of itself. It is a rare student who is always current on all assignments.

It is the circumstances (the A and C events in an ABC analysis) as well as the frequency, duration, and intensity of behavior that will help you determine whether a behavior constitutes a problem. The more you base your decisions on data about the behavior of interest, including normative information about appropriate and inappropriate behavior, the better decisions you are likely to make. As an example, consider the case of a student who has fallen behind in his studies. If a class project is late because it was not started on time, the problem may not be serious. On the other hand, if a student falls behind in his work time and time again, a problem does indeed exist.

Before proceeding with the plan, you must address two key ethical questions: Will a change in behavior serve the best interest of the person (her intellectual, physical, emotional, or social interests)? And will the most humane procedures possible be used?

The first question is related to setting appropriate and attainable goals, a topic of Chapter 3. The second is related to selecting reinforcing rather than aversive strategies for change, a topic discussed in Chapter 4. Any attempt to adequately discuss these and other ethical considerations in an abbreviated text of this type may itself be unethical. You are therefore urged to consult the references listed at the end of Part I, some of which provide helpful discussions of ethical issues and the responsible use of behavior change programming.

THE NINE-STEP PLAN IN PRACTICE

Most teachers and parents in every culture change their own and others' behavior quite easily and naturally with little or no awareness of the principles and practices presented in this book. But sometimes teachers and parents need help.

Consider the case of an elementary school teacher who was having problems controlling her students. The children were having difficulty going from one activity to another. The problem was especially evident during the transition from free play to storytime. The children simply ignored requests to put their toys away and settle down for storytime. They sometimes took 10 minutes or more to comply. The teacher unknowingly was rewarding problem behavior because she read stories to the children immediately after the long delays.

Since storytime was a strongly rewarding activity, the teacher decided on the following procedure. When free time came to an end, the room lights would be turned off for two minutes. When they were turned back on, all toys were to have been put away and everyone was to be sitting quietly, awaiting storytime. Should any child fail to comply with these requirements, storytime would be postponed to a time later in the day. (Note that this is a Type 2 punishment procedure and that the opportunity for a story was not eliminated for the entire day.) The teacher was to rehearse (roleplay positive and negative instances of the requirements) the new procedure several times before implementing it. She was also to intermittently praise the children for their efforts.

Implementation went smoothly and the plan was quite effective. Although the teacher was unaware of the general plan described here, all of its elements were used, as shown below.

THE NINE STEPS	DESCRIPTION
1. Define behavior	Toys put away, students sitting quietly.
2. Observe and record behavior	The problem occurred daily.
3. Set attainable goals	Children ready for storytime when the lights were turned on.
4. Identify potential rewards	Storytime was an established activity reward.
5. Select procedures	The positive reward (storytelling) was to follow appropriate behavior; also, praise for appropriate behavior was given by the teacher.

6. Rehearse procedures	This was done several times using roleplaying.
7. Implement plan	This was done after the roleplaying.
8. Monitor results	The plan was successful from the start.
9. Maintain gains	Teacher occasionally read additional stories as a reward for compliance; occasional praise was continued.

We began this chapter by pointing out that an ABC analysis is appropriate whenever we wish to change behavior in some deliberate and systematic way. The above episode can be interpreted in terms of this analysis. Before the behavior change plan was implemented, the teacher's directives (A events) were not very effective in getting students to put toys away and settle down for storytime (B events). The teacher was rewarding problem behaviors by reading stories after they occurred (C events). After the plan was implemented, the teacher's requests were associated with a new event, lights off (A events), while compliance with requests (B events) was rewarded with reading stories and teacher praise (C events). In effect, the teacher began rewarding appropriate rather than inappropriate behavior.

It would be nice if all situations requiring behavior change were as simple as this one. But they are not. Complex situations require greater concern for each step in the plan. The remaining chapters in Part I will focus on this nine-step plan for changing behavior.

SELF-QUIZ

This Self-Quiz covers several of the principles presented in this chapter. See if you can determine whether the following situations illustrate positive reinforcement, negative reinforcement, extinction, Type 1 punishment (positive punishment), Type 2 punishment (negative punishment), or none of these.

SITUATION	WRITE YOUR ANSWER HERE
1. Jason's parents ignored his questions about sex as he was growing up. Consequently, he keeps his questions about dating to himself.	____________
2. Wyman used to greet his colleague with friendly "hellos" and other similar expressions. Subsequently, Wyman's greetings were met with sarcastic comments. After several weeks of this, Wyman stopped speaking to his colleague.	____________

3. Sally's new jacket brought rave reviews. She now is seen wearing it more often. ______________

4. Joe teased Susan. She slapped him. ______________

5. When first married, Larry liked to do the grocery shopping. Almost invariably, though, he was criticized by his wife for forgetting items, paying too much, and so on. Consequently, he no longer shops for groceries. ______________

6. Because a student found classwork quite aversive (punishing), she began to spend a lot of time daydreaming. ______________

7. Whenever little Shannon jumped up and down on the sofa while watching TV, it was turned off for one minute. She stopped jumping after the TV had been turned off four times. ______________

Solutions

(1) Jason's parents have extinguished his inquiries about sex (attention was withheld). (2) Wyman stopped speaking to his colleague because speaking was followed by unfriendly comments (something was added), illustrating Type 1 punishment (positive punishment). (3) In Sally's case, positive reinforcement probably accounts for her wearing the new jacket more often (something was added and behavior increased). (4) Without more information, we do not know how the slap affected Joe's teasing, so we cannot say any principle is illustrated. Remember that a punisher, like a reinforcer, is identified by its effect on behavior, not by whether a stimulus or event looks like a punisher. (5) Type 1 punishment (positive punishment), nagging criticism, appears to have been the key factor in eliminating Larry's trips to the grocery store. (6) The student's daydreaming, at least initially, was negatively reinforced. Daydreaming served as an escape from classroom events that the student found aversive. (7) Finally, Type 2 punishment (negative punishment) accounts for the cessation of Shannon's jumping (something was subtracted and behavior stopped).

DEFINING BEHAVIOR

Before behavior can be observed in some deliberate and systematic way, it must be clearly defined. Many behaviors are relatively easy to define and observe, such as when a student calls out your name, repeats an error in long division, or asks a question. On the other hand, behaviors such as tattling, social withdrawal (shyness), aggression, noncompliance, and arguing are not so easy to define.

Consider tattling as an example. Suppose a student voluntarily keeps you informed about the whereabouts and activities of his classmates. It might occur to you that these reports amount to little more than tattling, so you decide to define the term. You will want to distinguish between tattling and other forms of reporting. You will also need to determine whether the student tattles to others as well as to you and whether only an occasional incident of tattling requires action on your part. Your definition might end up looking like this: "Tattling is making critical or complaining comments to me or others about what peers are doing more than once per day. Reporting that someone is hurt or in a dangerous situation is not tattling."

Definitions of behavior can be developed after observing a behavior in a variety of situations. In formulating a definition, it is important to focus on what a person *does* in those situations. In the case of social withdrawal, one might first observe the student in situations in which she avoids social contact. A definition of social withdrawal could then be developed by describing the specific behaviors judged to be withdrawal behaviors.

Assume that you are concerned with such a student, one who has minimal contact with others. Realizing that the characteristics associated with social withdrawal vary from person to person, you decide to observe the student in various situations over a period of several days. You judge the following behaviors to be indicative of social withdrawal: student goes to and from school alone; student spends free time by herself; student sits apart from others during lunch; student does not initiate conversation; and student does not volunteer answers in class.

Note that the first three behaviors may be indicative of social isolation or ostracism rather than withdrawal. You must consider, therefore, the conditions under which these behaviors occur—the A and C events in the ABC analysis discussed in Chapter 1. If, for example, a student tries to initiate social interaction but is rebuffed in her attempts, the problem may be ostracism, not withdrawal.

Characteristics of Good Definitions

There are three essential features of a good definition of behavior. The definition should (1) be clear and specific, (2) include all of the major components of the target behavior, and (3) be socially valid.

1. The definition should be clear and specific. This means that any number of people should be able to understand and apply your definition and agree that the behavior did or did not occur. You should be able to count the frequency of a target behavior during a certain period of time (how often it occurs in, say, 1 minute, 5 minutes, 30 minutes) or to determine the number of minutes or intervals of time in which the behavior occurred (Joey talked at least once in 60% of the 10-second intervals). Good definitions describe behaviors that can be seen, heard, or felt (touched). If terms are used that only infer or imply behaviors, they should be exchanged for terms that refer to directly observable action. Inferences about behavior are generally based on observations of particular behaviors that, collectively, account for making the inference in the first place. Let us say that "poor attitude" refers to making negative comments about a teacher, refusal to comply with instructions, and failure to complete assignments. In the interest of clarity and specificity, these specific behaviors should be addressed, rather than "poor attitude." Consider the definition of tattling given earlier. Although other definitions of tattling are possible, the one given appears to meet the criteria of clarity and specificity (making critical or complaining comments about what peers are doing). However, you can be certain of its adequacy only if the definition enables you and others to accurately determine when tattling occurs or does not occur.
2. The definition should include all of the major components of the target behavior, the observable behavior to be changed. Earlier, after a period of observation, five behaviors were judged to be indicative of social withdrawal. If these behaviors turned out to be the most important components of withdrawal for the particular student in question, then any definition based on these characteristics would be adequate with respect to this second criterion.
3. The definition should be socially valid. A socially valid definition is one that incorporates behaviors that are judged to be socially and educationally important. As an example, consider a student who occasionally slouches in his seat. If slouching is not harmful to him or others in any way, then the social validity of a definition requiring him to sit up straight at all times is open to question.

OBSERVING AND RECORDING BEHAVIOR

Defining socially valid behaviors so that others can agree that the behavior has or has not occurred is required before the target behavior can be changed in a systematic way. Once this is done (step 1 in the nine-step plan), you are ready to move to step 2, observing and recording behavior. Properly executed, step 2 will help you determine where and when a behavior occurs as well as estimate its current level or frequency. Thus, this step provides information for decision making and for evaluating the effectiveness of your behavior change plan after you implement it in step 7. This information is obtained by observing and recording the target behavior and then displaying the results in some easily understood manner such as on a chart or graph.

Product Recording. A product is an outcome (end result) of some behavior. Teachers have long known that valuable information about students is available by analyzing student products. For example, if you are concerned with misspelled words, you could count and record the number of misspelled words in a theme (the product) written by a student. Other familiar student products are worksheets, written homework assignments, drawings, written examinations, science specimens, recorded musical perform-ances, and so on. Product recording allows us to determine something about a person's behavior without being present or observing it when it occurred. In fact, we know something about Plato's thinking by reading his *Republic*, a product he left us over two thousand years ago.

Because correct answers are emphasized, student products are sometimes not analyzed as fully as they could be. In fact, many student products, such as essays and homework assignments, are returned without a mark on them other than a grade. Written comments on student products provide valuable information to improve student learning. Consider the scoring of a fourth-grader's responses to three-digit by two-digit multiplication problems. If a teacher merely marks the problems as correct or incorrect, important information about the student's approach to the algorithm is not recorded for further analysis or use by the teacher and student. Learning might well proceed more efficiently if the teacher marks not only the correct answer but also correct comma placement, multiplication by zero in the ones place, the placement of subproduct columns, and addition or regrouping errors.

It should be noted that many behaviors, such as classroom discussions or fighting, do not naturally leave a product to be analyzed. However, special equipment, such as video cameras, can be used to record these behaviors for later analysis. When it is not feasible to use equipment, the procedures discussed below allow you to observe and record behaviors. These procedures are called *direct observation* procedures because behavior is directly observed and recorded as it occurs. A number of direct observation procedures can be used, including narrative recording, frequency (event) recording, duration recording, latency recording, momentary time sampling, and interval recording.

Narrative Recording. Narrative recording is writing down all or most of a student's behavior as it occurs in a block of time, usually between 15 to 30 minutes. This technique is useful when you wish to develop a description of a student's general behavior pattern. Narrative recording is sometimes called *ABC recording* because it can provide information about behavior (B events) and what happened just before the behavior (A events) and immediately after it (C events). Analysis of narrative recordings can be very useful in deciding which behaviors are important, how they might be defined, and how best to observe them.

As an example of narrative recording, consider a student who has been described as "disruptive," but the nature of the disruptiveness is not clear. The student is then observed on one or more occasions in one or more classrooms or other locations. The observer records most of what the student does and most of what happens to him. Abbreviations and an invented shorthand are used in order to record as much as possible. Only what is seen and heard is recorded. No interpretation of the record is made at this time. Later, as you study and apply an ABC analysis to your written descriptions, you might discover that the student engages in three troublesome behaviors that account for the label "disruptiveness": arguing, swearing, and interrupting others. You might also discover, from your ABC analysis, that certain events happen just before the troublesome behavior (these events are said to *control* the behavior) and that certain events are consequences of the behavior (these events are said to *maintain* the behavior).

Frequency Recording. Frequency recording (sometimes called *event recording*), like product recording, is widely used by teachers. It involves counting or tallying directly observed discrete behaviors, behaviors that have a clear beginning and end (successive incidences of behavior are similar in duration). This technique is easy to use and can provide accurate information about behavior. Examples of frequency recording include counting the number of times a student hits, swears, interrupts, tattles, volunteers, makes self-references, or compliments others. When teachers record the number (frequency) of correct answers on a quiz (product), they are using product recording because the target behavior occurred earlier.

It is sometimes necessary to consider not only the number of times a behavior occurs but also the amount of time you spent observing it. Suppose that you observed a student hit others 10 times during a 30-minute period on the first day of your observations. On the second day, you spent fifty minutes observing the student and noted that he hit others only five times. Because the amount of time you spent observing was different for the two days, you must consider the rate of hitting instead of the number of times hitting occurred. Response rate is determined by dividing the number of responses (in our example, it is "hitting others") by the amount of time (minutes, in our example) the responses were observed. Thus, on the first day, the response rate was .33 per minute (10 divided by 30). Response rate on the second day was 0.10 per minute (5 divided by 50). Thus, the student's rate of hitting was higher on the first day.

Duration Recording. In duration recording, one notes how long behavior lasts. Many everyday behaviors are measured along a temporal dimension. Duration is recorded to determine the cost of our long-distance telephone calls. Log time on a computer is also a measure of duration. People often tell others how long it took to do certain tasks. They might say, "Jill practiced the violin 20 minutes today," "I went for a two-hour walk," "The dinner took four hours to prepare," or "Micah watches television five hours a day." Teachers can use duration recording to determine, for example, time spent reading, throwing tantrums, being off-task, and staring into space.

Latency Recording. Latency is also a temporal measure of behavior. With this technique, the elapsed time between the onset of a signal or cue and the student's response to it is recorded. Thus, latency recording is a very appropriate measure when teachers are concerned with compliance or with the time it takes a student to begin a task after a request is made. Chapter 1 described an elementary school teacher who had a compliance problem in her classroom; students were taking 10 minutes or more to respond to her requests to move on from one activity to another.

Momentary Time Sampling. In momentary time sampling, a period of time is divided into manageable units or intervals (e.g., 5, 10, 15, 20 minutes). Then the target behavior is momentarily observed at the end of each interval to determine if the behavior occurred or not. For example, a teacher might take a few seconds at the end of every 15 minutes to count the number of students who are on- or off-task, in- or out-of-seat, or talking without permission. Parents who occasionally check the play area to see whether all is well with their children are informally using momentary time sampling. Note that one observes only some incidents of behavior, those that occur at the end of prespecified periods of time. Time sampling is rather easy to use (a watch can be set to sound a low tone at prespecified intervals) and can be applied with little or no interference in your daily activities.

Interval Recording. In interval recording, a period of time is divided into units or intervals that are often smaller than those used in momentary time sampling (e.g., 10, 20, 30, 60 seconds). The observer then determines whether the target behavior occured during each interval. Note that the observer actually records the number of intervals in which a behavior occurs rather than the frequency of the behavior itself. Because interval recording requires continuous observation, the busy teacher will find its use impractical, unless someone else does the observing and recording.

You are advised to construct appropriate data-collection sheets when you use the above observational systems. For example, your data sheet for frequency recording might resemble the simple format shown in Figure 2-1.

FIGURE 2-1 Sample Data Sheet for Frequency Recording

Name: *Jan* Date: *9/1/89* Target Behavior: *Talking without permission*

Time: *10 10* Start: *10 15* Stop: *10:40*

Place a check for each occurrence: ✓✓✓✓✓✓✓✓✓✓✓✓✓✓✓✓✓

Total number of occurrences: *17*

Figure 2-2 shows part of a suggested data-collection sheet for interval recording. A plus indicates an occurrence of the target behavior. A zero indicates a nonoccurrence. Figure 2-2 shows a record for a student who was off-task during 60% of the 10-second intervals in a 5-minute period of time.

FIGURE 2-2 Sample Data Sheet for Interval Recording

	1	+	o	o	+	+	+
	2	+	o	o	o	o	+
Minutes	3	+	+	+	+	+	+
	4	+	o	o	+	+	o
	5	o	o	o	+	+	+
		1	2	3	4	5	6

10-second Intervals

Because there are a variety of observational systems from which to choose, you may find some general guidelines helpful. In the final analysis, however, you will have to do a little experimenting to determine which observational procedure will work best for you.

Remember to count behavior whenever you can (frequency recording). You can probably count the number of derogatory comments made, assignments completed, pages read, sentences written, problems solved, and paper wads thrown. But frequency recording is not appropriate when behavior occurs so quickly that you cannot count it accurately, such as the number of self references made by a student who talks very fast. It is also inappropriate when you do not have time to devote to this kind of observation or when the target behavior is continuous rather than discrete, such as when someone is watching a movie, reading, working on-task, playing, or being overactive. Consider duration recording when you are concerned with how long a behavior lasts (talking, being off-task, staring into space) and latency recording when you are interested in elapsed time before a student responds (being late, complying with directives). Momentary time sampling is a convenient procedure to use when the target behavior occurs at a moderately high rate or when you are unable to count the behavior. Because behavior is observed only momentarily at the end of prespecified time periods, it is not an appropriate procedure to use for behaviors that seldom occur. Finally, consider using interval recording when behavior occurs at a rate too high to count accurately, when behavior is continuous, and when someone is available to help you observe.

Which ever observational system you use, you may want to check the reliability or accuracy of your observations from time to time. This requires a second person to observe the behavior of the same student at the same time you do. These observations should be entirely independent of yours.

Suppose you count a total of 20 instances of swearing during a 50-minute period. Someone else, a colleague or student, counts 18 incidents during the same time period. A practical way to determine the accuracy of your observations is to calculate the percent of time you and the other observer agree. This can be done by dividing the smaller number of observed incidents by the larger number and multiplying the result by 100. Thus, in the above case, the percent of agreement is 90% (18 divided by 20, then multiplied by 100). If you are using duration or latency recording,

FIGURE 2-3 Interval Recording Record of Two Observers

Observer A	+	o	o	+	+
Observer B	+	o	+	o	+
	1	2	3	4	5

Intervals

divide the lowest number of minutes by the larger number. A similar procedure is appropriate for momentary time sampling and interval recording. In these cases, divide the number of intervals in which the observers agree by the total number of intervals used in the observations. Sometimes greater accuracy can be achieved by excluding from your calculations those intervals in which neither observer records the behavior. Figure 2-3 shows that the observers agreed with respect to intervals 1, 2, and 5. Thus, the percent of agreement is 60% (3 divided by 5, then multiplied by 100).

Ordinarily you should settle for nothing less than 80% agreement. If your observations do not reach this level, your behavioral definition may be imprecise or the observers may need to sharpen their observational skills.

DISPLAYING THE RESULTS OF YOUR OBSERVATIONS

It may be profitable to take a moment to review the behavior change plan up to this point. Remember, in step 1, you must define the behavior of interest (the target behavior) in clear and objective terms. In step 2, using the definition from step 1, you observe the target behavior and record your findings using one or more of the methods discussed. The result is a record of the target behavior over a period of time. At this point in the plan, you should display the information you have collected in a simple graph or chart. There are several advantages to such a display:

1. Graphs and charts enable us to see at a glance a student's performance over an extended period of time.
2. Plotting behavior on graphs or charts helps diminish a tendency to interpret slight variations in performance as more important than they are. Sometimes, when changes in behavior are analyzed statistically, "significant" changes in behavior may have little practical value.
3. The information on a graph or chart can have an important influence on the student whose performance is displayed.

The third advantage needs some elaboration. Because people do not often carefully observe their own or others' behavior, observational data can have important motivational properties. Simply recording behavior can be instrumental in changing it. Consider the example of a couple and their son, who was known to be highly aggressive in school. Up to the time that data were collected, the parents denied the seriousness of the problem. In fact, there was a near total breakdown in communication between home and school. When the parents and their son were shown a simple graph of the number of aggressive incidents across 10 school days, they changed their view of things rather drastically. It was hard to deny good, systematic data. Subsequent intervention was quite successful, due in no small way to this change in parental perspective.

The term *baseline* refers to the target behavior before intervention. In the case of aggression cited above, the number of aggressive acts for 10 school days is *baseline data.* Baseline data allow you to determine what effect, if any, your change strategies are having on the target behavior, since you will be comparing the student's behavior during your intervention with the student's behavior prior to intervention. Observing and recording current or baseline behavior may take a few seconds or several days, depending on its variability. There would be no need to establish a baseline (recording behavior prior to intervention) for the completion of homework assignments if, for example, a student has not turned in an assignment for several weeks. On the other hand, many behaviors—such as verbal abuse, level of academic performance, and athletic skill—may fluctuate from day to day. In these cases, you may need to observe behavior over several sessions to establish baselines.

Let us look at a hypothetical example to summarize. Suppose a teacher is concerned about a student who verbally abuses others. The student, Vinney, calls his classmates names ("nerd", "fatso") and keeps up a steady stream of derogatory remarks ("Look at the mop he calls his hair!" "Put a bag over it, honey!"). After the teacher defines *verbal abuse,* he decides to collect baseline data. He decides to observe Vinney during third-period class when his rate of verbal abuse seems to be highest.

The teacher observed the following number of incidents over five days: 15, 6, 6, 16, and 17. Because he was a busy teacher, the length of the observation periods were unequal. Thus, the number of observations are better presented as response rate than as response frequency. The teacher recorded his observations on a card such as the one shown in Figure 2–4.

FIGURE 2-4 Response Card for Vinney

Name: Vinney
Behavior: Verbal abuse; name calling; making derogatory comments
Where/When: English class; third period
Probable Reinforcers: Social; attention from others; students respond defensively

Day	Frequency	Time	Rate per Minute
2-8	15	10:00–10:50	.30
2-9	6	10:10–10:30	.30
2-10	6	10:05–10:35	.20
2-11	16	10:18–10:50	.50
2-12	17	10:05–10:47	.40

We can get an overall visual impression of these baseline data by placing them on a graph. In Figure 2–5, frequency of verbal abuse is shown on the left graph and rate of verbal abuse on the right. You can see that the two

FIGURE 2-5 Graphs of Frequency and Rate of Verbal Abuse

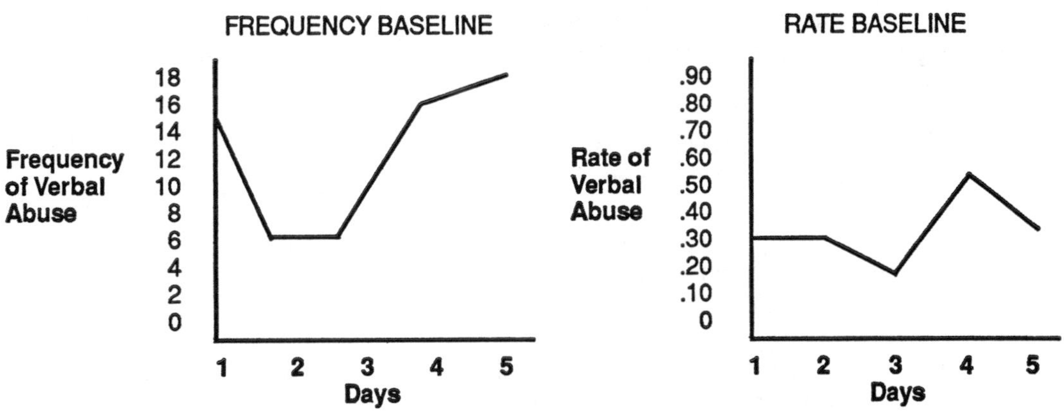

graphs of the same behavior differ considerably. The frequency graph is, in fact, misleading. It shows a decrease in verbal abuse from the first to the second day when its rate actually remained the same. This is because graphing frequency is appropriate only when the opportunity for behavior to occur and the time in which to observe it are comparable from one session to another. The point is clear: Report response rate rather than frequency when opportunity and time are not nearly constant from one observation period to the next.

As a point of interest, when you make a graph, behavior (its frequency or rate) is plotted on the vertical line (ordinate), whereas sessions (in minutes, hours, days, and so on) are plotted on the horizontal line (abscissa).

SELF-QUIZ

Determine which type of observational recording is most appropriate for the situations below.

SITUATION	WRITE YOUR ANSWER HERE
1. Jamie interrupts others on numerous occasions. He simply doesn't wait for them to complete a sentence or statement before he begins talking.	____________________
2. Sue makes a lot of spelling errors. Her teacher doesn't know whether a pattern of errors exists or whether particular words give Sue the most difficulty.	____________________
3. Paul is constantly out of his seat for long periods without permission.	____________________
4. Stacy leaves his seat for short periods (15 to 20 seconds) without permission throughout the day. This disturbs others.	____________________
5. Trace hums to himself 3 or 4 times each day. He seems to be unaware of his humming.	____________________
6. Ms. Peters thinks her students take too long to line up when asked.	____________________

7. Billy is almost always late to class after lunch. He claims that he is a slow eater and doesn't have enough time to finish. His teacher suspects that delays going to the cafeteria are the problem. ____________________

8. A colleague tells you that her class is in constant turmoil. She invites you in to observe. ____________________

9. Mr. Gomez is concerned about the amount of talking that bursts forth in his classroom, especially in the afternoon. He wants to present some hard evidence before he talks with his students about the problem. ____________________

Solutions

(1) Frequency recording can be used to observe Jamie's interruptions. (2) Sue's teacher needs to collect and analyze several of Sue's spelling assignments (products). (3) & (4) Duration or time sampling should work in Paul's case, while frequency recording is appropriate for Stacy's problem. Although both Paul and Stacy leave their seats, Paul's out-of-seat behavior is continuous, while Stacy's can be treated as discrete behavior since it has a clear beginning and end and each instance extends over a short period of time. (5) Trace's humming incidents can be counted (frequency recording). Duration recording might also be appropriate if Trace's humming extends over long intervals. However, because of its low rate, time sampling would be inappropprate. (6) Ms. Peters should try latency recording. The behavior in this episode is lining up which has yet to occur; thus, duration (how long a behavior lasts) would be inappropriate. (7) Billy's delays can be observed by taking a measure of latency (from the bell signaling lunch to his arrival in the cafeteria). (8) Because you don't know the nature of your colleague's concerns, narrative recording may help you determine problem areas in her classroom. (9) Mr. Gomez can use duration, interval recording, or momentary time sampling (for instance, checking after 10-minute intervals) to collect his hard evidence.

CHAPTER 3 / SETTING ATTAINABLE GOALS AND IDENTIFYING POTENTIAL REWARDS

SETTING ATTAINABLE GOALS

After you have a clear definition of the target behavior and an estimate of its current or baseline level, you will need to answer the question: What can I realistically expect the behavior to look like after intervention?

The answer to this question constitutes the attainable goal for your behavior change project. Some answers will come to you easily, some not. For example, should physical aggression be reduced to zero or near-zero levels? In almost all cases, the obvious answer is yes. But what about completing homework assignments? Should all students complete all assignments, even a student who currently does no assignments? And how often should a socially withdrawn student initiate conversation?

The answers to these questions are not so obvious. The following guidelines may assist you in setting goals for behavior change.

1. Set goals that are attainable and in the best interest of the student. Some students will not excel in academics or become highly skilled athletes no matter what you do. Goals that are set too high or too low are not in the best interest of the student.
2. Involve students in goal setting. When students have a part in setting personal goals, they are more likely to strive to attain them. In the process, they might well take a step toward greater independence.
3. Reward the student in a series of small steps leading to the goal. This procedure will minimize the aversive consequences that occur when teachers compare a student's performance with that of advanced students or with criteria that are too high. Rewarding small gains makes learning motivating because the student is rewarded at every step for doing what he or she is able to do at that point.

IDENTIFYING POTENTIAL REWARDS AS MOTIVATORS

Motivation is a concept that covers a broad spectrum of concerns, ranging from genetic and physiological factors to so-called psychogenic and cognitive motives. For behavior change programs within a school environment, as discussed in this book, it is best to view motivation practically in terms of reinforcement. As you seek potential motivators (reinforcers), keep in mind the categories of reinforcers that were mentioned in Chapter 1 and that are discussed below.

A social reinforcer is any act by a person—such as a smile, a spoken word, a gesture, a hug—that follows someone's behavior and strengthens it in the sense that the target behavior is more likely to occur again. Thus, teachers influence the likelihood of many kinds of student performance when they follow a behavior with a pat on the back, words of praise, or other forms of recognition and attention. When students ask to sit by a friend, lead a group, or publish their article in the school newspaper, they are, at least in part, asking for social reinforcers.

An activity reinforcer is a behavior that strengthens another behavior that it follows. Activities that can function as reinforcers include free time, early dismissal from school, TV watching, running errands, tutoring peers, reading, painting, daydreaming, access to computers, doing crossword puzzles, and playing games.

The systematic use of activity reinforcers is sometimes referred to as the Premack Principle. This very important principle allows us to identify reinforcers without knowing very much about a student's previous learning history. The principle can be stated in this way: When one activity is preferred over another, the preferred activity may be used to reinforce the less preferred, or less likely, activity. For example, a teacher might grant access to free time or to a computer to reinforce a student for doing something he is less likely to do, such as completing a map-reading assignment or refraining from an undesirable act.

Let's consider an actual example of how the Premack Principle was applied in a resource-room setting where the students were said to be unmotivated. Even though the students were not completing many assignments, they were allowed access to several highly motivitating activities, including video cassettes and games. Motivation to complete tasks increased markedly simply by making access to the preferred activities contingent on completing assignments.

This little example serves to illustrate another important principle: If students like certain activities, you need only change *when* the activities are provided to change behavior. In the example, those activities already in the resource room were used to motivate the students. The major change was *when* they were provided.

A tangible reinforcer is a physical, nonedible object. Some tangible reinforcers include marks of progress (grades, "smiley faces," gain scores on a chart), awards, trinkets, books and magazines, points or tokens to be exchanged for other reinforcers, and coupons for restaurants and sports events.

A primary reinforcer is one that is necessary for the survival of the species, such as food, water, and sensory stimulation. You should use primary reinforcers sparingly, especially when activity, social, and tangible reinforcers are readily available.

The following suggestions will help you locate reinforcers that might serve to motivate students.

- Watch what a student does in a variety of settings. Students who spend a lot of free time talking, dancing, drawing, listening to music, reading, playing tennis, watching television, shopping, lifting weights, shooting rockets, or collecting things are, by their actions, telling you what they like to do. These activities might be used in an application of the Premack Principle.
- Take note of the student's friends, including the adults in his life. These people may be able to provide some social support for behavior change.
- Interview the student, as well as others who know her well. Keeping in mind the reward categories, ask a series of gently probing questions in each category. You should end up with lists of possible reinforcers for each category. In fact, interviewing a student, her mother, and a former teacher will yield 12 lists in all, if each person can name at least one reinforcer in each of the four categories.
- Success and signs of progress are powerful motivators for almost everyone. Students are rewarded when they see that they can do something today (academically, artistically, athletically) that they could not do yesterday. Therefore, try to provide plenty of simple records (charts, graphs) that let students see their progress. This suggestion, of course, applies to all students, the advanced as well as the less advanced.
- Watch for the payoffs that follow persistent misbehavior. Some students do not seem to be motivated by academic achievement, teacher praise, and so on. Yet anyone who engages in problem behavior (swearing, cheating, talking without permission, annoying others) day in and day out is getting rewarded for that behavior, at least some of the time. Try applying an ABC analysis to determine what these rewards might be. For example, is someone reinforcing the student's misbehavior by giving in to it and, in turn, being negatively reinforced for giving in (something annoying is removed)?
- You might get some leads about rewards for a given student by noting what his close friends and associates enjoy doing.
- Try reinforcer sampling. Perhaps you have sampled some food in a supermarket and found yourself buying it. Or perhaps you have watched an entire television program because you were attracted by one of the several segments that were introduced at the beginning of the program. In a like manner, let your students sample part of an educational game and other activities. If they find some of the samples attractive, access to the activities might function as rewards later.

SELF-QUIZ

Read the episodes given below and identify possible rewards (social, activity, or tangible) that might serve as motivators.

EPISODES	WRITE YOUR ANSWER HERE
1. Ms. Jacobson notices Betty Sue humming and singing during recess. During free time in the classroom, she prefers to listen to records and discuss the "top 40" hits with her friends.	______________________
2. Ed often brings to class model airplanes that he makes at home. He is very knowledgeable about the planes he makes and once earned a prize for the best model in his Boy Scout troop.	______________________
3. Mrs. Jamerson noticed that Elverna likes to receive funny stickers on the papers she turns in. She collects stickers and has made a notebook with different types of stickers in it.	______________________
4. Bev seems to thrive on being with others. She is very popular with her peers and does more than her share of talking with others, often without permission.	______________________
5. In a recent parent-teacher conference, Mr. Walker learned, much to his surprise, that Marcus volunteers his Saturdays to help tend the animals at the humane center.	______________________

Solutions

(1) & (2) Betty Sue and Ed would probably be motivated by activity rewards. Betty Sue could be allowed to listen privately to a personal Walkman with a cassette she could bring from home. Ed could be given free time to work on a model of his choice. Later he could make a report to the class about the plane that he made. (3) Elverna obviously likes a tangible reinforcer. Her teacher could continue to use stickers as special rewards for appropriate tasks. (4) Simply having a few minutes of "talk time" with others might provide social reinforcement for Bev. (5) For Marcus, taking care of a class pet (an activity), such as a gerbil, would seem to be highly motivating to him.

SOME PRELIMINARY CONCERNS

If you have followed our suggestions for identifying reinforcers given in Chapter 3, you now have a list of possible rewards from which to choose. The intervention strategies discussed in this chapter provide a means to deliver these reinforcers. But before any strategies are applied, you must consider several principles for selecting and using reinforcers.

Selecting Reinforcers

Keep these principles in mind when selecting reinforcers.

1. Remember that events that function as reinforcers for one student may not do so for another. The section on motivation in Chapter 3 will help you locate potential reinforcers for individual students.
2. Select reinforcers to which the student has little or no access. Some degree of deprivation is necessary if something is to function as a reinforcer. People are not likely to be motivated by food, for instance, if they have just eaten a big meal. Similarly, if a student likes computers and has free access to them apart from your intervention plan, you are not likely to motivate her by offering additional time on the computer. Ideally, only you should control access to the rewards in your program. If control is not possible, you can either find a way to diminish the student's access to a reward (e.g., ask her parents to limit access at home), or select other reinforcers from your list.
3. Select reinforcers that are compatible with your instructional goals. For instance, one teacher attempted to get an "emotionally disturbed" adolescent male interested in reading. She asked him to select a book from a list of "exciting" books she had prepared. The student picked a popular book about torture and murder! Obviously, the teacher's choice of books to place on a reading list was highly questionable for an emotionally disturbed person. Selecting appropriate reinforcers requires some common sense as well as informed planning.
4. Avoid controversial reinforcers. Some parents, for example, might object to the use of candy or money as motivators. Try building as many social and activity reinforcers as you can into your intervention program.

Using Reinforcers

Remember the following principles when using reinforcers.

1. Be clear about the behavior to be changed. Defining behavior clearly will improve the chances of reinforcing performance in a consistent manner.
2. Tell the student how reinforcement will work ("If you do that, then you will earn ..."). Instructions should speed up the learning process for those who understand them.
3. Reinforce behavior while it is occurring or immediately after it occurs. It would be difficult to exaggerate the fundamental importance of this principle. Its misapplication can lead to many problems, as illustrated by an episode with Juan. Juan was finally at work on his geometry assignment after several days of idleness. He received no recognition for his efforts while he worked. He stopped after 20 minutes and began clowning with a classmate. While he was clowning, his teacher said, "Juan, it's great that you got down to work on your geometry." If the teacher's remark functioned as a reinforcer, we can see that the principle of immediacy had been misapplied. She actually reinforced clowning. The principle of immediacy would be violated even if Juan had not engaged in clowning. In this case, the teacher would reinforce stopping (idleness), the problem behavior itself.
4. Reward small gains. Remember that behavior must occur for it to be reinforced. If you require large gains, you will reduce the number of opportunities to reinforce the student and may discourage her as well.
5. When the behavior of interest occurs, reinforce it frequently. Thus, the more frequently you reinforce performance during initial stages of learning, the more the desired behavior will occur.
6. Take steps to prevent satiation. Satiation is the opposite of deprivation. When a person repeatedly receives a reinforcer, the reinforcer (food, novel stimuli, talking with a friend) may lose its effectiveness, at least temporarily. The likelihood of satiation can be reduced by (a) using small amounts of the reinforcer, (b) allowing the student to select from a variety of reinforcers, (c) scheduling short teaching sessions, if appropriate, and (d) by using points or tokens to be exchanged for other reinforcers later.
7. After the target behavior becomes well established, gradually make reinforcement less and less frequent (this is called thinning the reinforcement schedule). Occasional or intermittent reinforcement should suffice at this point.

With these important principles in mind, we now consider some specific strategies for changing behaviors.

STRATEGIES FOR INCREASING BEHAVIORS

The first four strategies focus on events that are antecedent to student behavior and are sometimes easier to apply than the others. If appropriate, try them first. But whether you select from these or other strategies, be consistent in your application of the strategies. Inconsistent application of ethically and pedagogically sound procedures may do more harm than good. Stay with your plan until you are reasonably clear about why it is not working. Remember that things may not run smoothly for the first few applications of the intervention.

1. *Instruction.* One form of instruction involves the presentation of spoken or written words that describe what a person is to do. Thus, "Write a title for the passage you just read," "Turn in your worksheets before you leave," and "Right, face!" are instances of instruction. A person can instruct himself (self-instruction), such as "Slow down, you're talking too fast" or "*I* before *e* except after *c*." Although instruction exerts a powerful and efficient influence on behavior, its exclusive use can be counterproductive. Saying "I think you should thank people when they do something nice for you" will work with some students but not others. When this happens, the teacher must turn to more effective methods or combine instruction and other strategies.

Effective instruction (teaching) is, of course, a very complex topic. Students presented with a poorly defined curriculum, weak teaching strategies, and an inadequate classroom structure are likely to display aberrant behaviors. Situations where effective instruction is practiced will have fewer behavior problems.

Although the broad topic of teaching is beyond the scope of this text, major elements of effective instruction can at least be mentioned. Effective instruction generally involves the following:

(a) Instructional programming based on a sophisticated analysis of the knowledge sets to be taught.
(b) Clearly stated instructional objectives.
(c) Task analyses of the stated objectives and their presentation at curriculum levels in which all prerequisite skills have been attained.
(d) Instructional sequencing in small steps to minimize failure and to maximize success. Good programs let students see progress day by day and, consequently, provide motivation to learn.
(e) Frequent student responding and frequent feedback for these responses (rather than merely listening or reading). Students perform what they are to learn.
(f) Student performance, with frequent appropriate feedback, across various response options, including oral reports, writing activities, and individual and group projects.
(g) Full recognition that students learn at different rates, as reflected in program changes in light of student progress and in program flexibility to allow for differential learning time.

(h) Remedial help for those who need it.
(i) Provisions for assessing retention.

2. *Situational changes.* The setting in which behavior occurs has a profound influence on it. Consider the differences in people's behavior in church versus at a party or before and after the advent of television. Advertisers compete to place their goods near the checkout counter in a supermarket, and the management of fast-food restaurants has long known that uncomfortable furniture hastens customers in and out. Teachers, too, can alter the classroom setting to bring about a wide range of behavioral changes as these examples illustrate.

    - Because Mr. Jones's students had to request toys and materials (he deliberately placed them out of reach), they have increased their use of language.
    - Ms. Powers posted a new requirement for essay questions: "No writing, only outlining, for the first 15 minutes of the exam." She has noted distinct improvements in the organization and clarity of student essays.
    - Sylvia has made great strides in arithmetic since her teacher gave her supplementary (programmed) materials to work on.
    - Elizabeth is studying much more successfully since study areas free from distractions have been set up for her in school and at home.
    - Ms. Legrande has switched a highly motivating activity from the morning to the afternoon schedule. The rescheduling has eliminated the afternoon doldrums that have plagued her sixth-period class all year.

3. *Prompting and fading.* A *prompt* is a cue or supplemental stimulus to help a student respond to a new stimulus. *Fading* is the gradual elimination of the cue or supplemental stimulus. A teacher can help a student learn to write the letters of the alphabet by using prompts. The teacher might first present the letters as a series of dotted lines with these instructions: "Trace the letter with your pencil. Start here." When the student learns to trace a completely dotted letter (prompt), the student is given letters with fewer and fewer dots (fading) until he can write letters with no prompts. Teaching will someday make much greater use of sophisticated prompting and fading. When this happens, education will take a very large step toward greater efficiency. Fewer errors in learning a task allows more time to learn something else. Some examples of prompting are given below.

    - *Verbal prompting.* When drama students forget their lines, another student cues them from off stage.
    - *Physical prompting.* A tennis coach guides his student's arm and wrist as he helps him learn proper backhand form.
    - *Pictorial prompting.* A posted rule in social studies is "Quiet, please." These words are accompanied by a picture of a woman holding her index finger across her lips.

- *Gestural prompting.* A basketball coach positions his players by pointing to where they should be on the court during play.
- *Mechanical prompting.* A female gymnast is guided by a beep sound each time part of her body strays too far off the perpendicular during practice on the balance beam.

Teachers should fade prompts as soon as possible to avoid the danger of students becoming dependent on them. An important instructional goal for the gymnast, for example, is good performance without the aid of the beeper.

4. *Modeling.* People are influenced in subtle and not so subtle ways by what they observe others say and do. The person who provides a sample of behavior to others is *modeling* some behavior. Those who observe the model's actions and behave similarly are engaging in *imitative* action. Much of our appropriate and inappropriate behavior is learned by imitating the behavior of models. Models are observed both directly and symbolically (as presented on television, in books, and so on). Students imitate their teacher's pronunciation of words or their solutions to algebra problems, the golf swing of their coach, the clothing styles seen on television, and the aggressive actions of parents or peers. Modeling is especially efficient when it is combined with various forms of instruction.

   Students are likely to engage in imitative behavior when (a) they are rewarded for attending and imitating the model's actions, a critical component of the early stages of imitation; (b) they perceive the model's actions as leading to reinforcement or the avoidance of punishment; and (c) they see similarities between the model and themselves. (Student athletes, for example, are more likely to imitate the athletic behavior of other athletes than the behavior of unathletic people.)
5. *Differentially Reinforce Alternative behavior (DRA).* DRA is a procedure whereby one behavior (the target behavior) is selectively reinforced while other behaviors are ignored. DRA is used when more than one response is possible but only one is selected for reinforcement. A teacher is using DRA when she marks one answer "right" and ignores other answers on a multiple-choice question. She is also using the procedure when she acknowledges constructive criticism while ignoring whining and complaining. DRA is the premier strategy for changing performance. Use it whenever you can.
6. *Successive approximation (Shaping).* Successive approximation, also called *shaping*, is a procedure by which a new behavior (one the student cannot now perform) is learned by rewarding responses as they get closer and closer to a target behavior. It is changing behavior small step by small step. Shaping is not recommended when instruction, situational changes, prompting, or modeling will bring about the desired changes. Consider this illustration:

- Darrell has had a long history of failure associated with writing. In fact, he can hardly write a correct sentence, not to mention a paragraph, personal letter, or theme. His new teacher, Mrs. Trout, decided to teach Darrell to write by rewarding small gains toward the goal of writing correct personal letters of at least one paragraph in length. She first rewarded

Darrell for each correct word he wrote. He had little trouble with this. Darrell then moved on to two-word responses. Mrs. Trout provided plenty of attention, praise, and feedback for small gains along the way. Before long, Darrell was producing a sentence, then sentences, then paragraphs, and, finally, a well-written letter. Darrell's case will serve as a reference as the essential features of successive approximation are outlined.

(a) Determine the target behavior. In Darrell's case, it was writing correct personal letters of a certain length. (b) Select possible reinforcers. Effective reinforcers for Darrell were the teacher's praise, enthusiasm about his responses, and signs of progress (feedback). (c) Require active responding. Darrell made a large number of responses on his way to the target behavior. (d) Provide immediate reinforcement. Mrs. Trout provided plenty of reinforcement, especially at the beginning of each successive step. (e) Use successive approximation. Darrell was first rewarded for *doing what he could already do* (i.e., write single words). The task was broken down into small enough units so that he could experience success at each step. (f) Change criteria for reinforcement. Darrell remained at a step until he learned that particular step. Only then did he move on to the next approximation.

7. *Contracting.* A contract is an agreement between two or more people that specifies a relationship between behavior and consequences. The relationship is usually in terms of "if/then." For example, a contract might say, "If you complete at least 80% of your daily assignment in math, then you may work on your television project for 15 minutes at the end of the day." Contracts are usually written and signed by the participants. They have been applied to a wide range of problem areas, including truancy, fighting, arguing, drug abuse, and failure to complete tasks. They are especially useful in bringing people together to discuss problems and their solutions, in providing a record of who promised what to whom, and in supporting student commitment to change (commiting oneself in front of others often strengthens the commitment). Consider the recommendations given below for writing contracts.

Put contracts in writing. Keep them as simple as possible. Specify attainable performance ("Tim will complete all homework in arithmetic with at least 80% accuracy"). Specify the rewards and privileges for attainment ("Each completed assignment is worth five points. Points can be exchanged for additional allowance, choice of Sunday dinner, television time, trip to Chicago with Dad, and so on"). Some activities and items, of course, require more points than others. Emphasize positive requirements ("Tim will complete ..." rather than "If Tim fails to complete ..."). State who will deliver the rewards and when. Identify possible problems and plans for solutions ("If Tim has difficulty completing an assignment, he can ask Mom or Dad for help"). Specify minor penalities for noncompliance ("Tim will bring his book and homework from school each time an assignment is made or else he will owe 3 points"). Include bonus plans for when the student goes "beyond the call of duty" ("Tim will earn an extra point each time he reviews an earlier assignment. Dad will supervise this review"). Sign and date each contract. Keep careful records of progress (a critical component).

It is also a good idea to specify a time span for each contract. Initial contracts should be of short duration (two to five days) so that flaws can be corrected as soon as possible. The time span for subsequent contracts can be gradually lengthened as progress permits. Try to design contracts so that rewards are delivered immediately and frequently, at least for the first few contracts. Contracts should be honest in the sense that all parties must honor the contract when it is in effect. Opportunities for negotiation and renegotiation should be provided, and all parties should perceive the contract as fair.

8. *Token reinforcement.* Tokens (e.g., points, stars, plastic coins) are generalized reinforcers that can be exchanged for other reinforcers called *backup reinforcers.* A token reinforcement system has much in common with the use of money in our daily economy. In fact, it is appropriate to call such a system a token economy. Although points are emphasized here, what follows applies to tokens as well as any other similar medium of exchange.

   Three features characterize a point (or token) system: (1) points to be exchanged, (2) backup rewards, and (3) rules that specify the relationships between the specific behaviors that earn points and the backup reinforcers for which the points are exchanged. Here is a very simple point system: Chris will receive a point for each worksheet completed satisfactorily. Points may be exchanged for 10-minute breaks (3 points each), study periods in Ms. Kuo's room (5 points each), and a ticket to next week's basketball game (10 points). Since point systems work only when backup rewards are appealing to students, try to provide a wide range of social, activity, and tangible rewards from which to choose.

   Point or token programs have been implemented widely in classrooms and other settings because they are generally quite effective when conceived and administered with care. Such programs have several advantages: (a) because points can be delivered immediately, they help bridge delays between performance and the delivery of other kinds of reinforcers; (b) backup reinforcers allow students to express individual preferences; (c) because of their generalized nature, points are resistant to satiation effects.

STRATEGIES FOR REDUCING BEHAVIORS

Before listing some of the procedures for reducing behavior, several very important points must be made. First, the strategies for the reduction of behavior are presented in order of preference. Note that the beginning strategies focus on events antecedent to behavior (level 1). The discussion then moves on to reinforcement techniques (level 2). Only then are extinction procedures (level 3) and punishment procedures (level 4) presented.

When selecting strategies to reduce student behaviors, start with the first two strategies (these are sometimes referred to as "shortcut" methods), and, if necessary, work your way down the list. Refrain from applying exclusionary time out, overcorrection, negative practice, and contingent effort (level 4 procedures), unless you have tried or seriously considered the previous strategies. In any event, you are advised to enlist professional assistance when applying punishment.

Second, the goal of good behavior change programming is not simply to supress inappropriate behavior but rather to build alternative, adaptive performance. For example, consider a student who is persistently out of her seat. Why do we want her to remain seated? To comply with a rule or to provide an opportunity for her to learn? The basic reason, of course, is to provide an opportunity to learn. In Part II of this text, we highlight this concern by identifying some alternative behaviors for each behavior problem discussed.

The discussion that follows largely ignores many of the strategies used routinely by some teachers, including corporal punishment, scolding, suspension from school, sending students to the principal's office, writing sentences ("I will not talk without permission"), lowering grades in a subject area, and assigning additional academic work for misbehavior. These time-honored techniques presumably pay off in some way, else they would not persist in our schools. But what are the pedagogical and psychological costs of relying on such techniques?

This text has not focused on such disciplinary techniques for three related reasons. First, when they work to reduce behavior, they are forms of punishment. As such, they are level 4 procedures and at the bottom of the preference list specified above. Second, some of the techniques are highly questionable on pedagogical grounds. For example, is it pedagogically defensible to contaminate a student's grade, say, in geometry by reducing it for disciplinary rather than academic reasons? And should a teacher ever deliberately use academic work as *punishment* for misbehavior? Third, whether or not the above procedures work, there is a risk that their use will elicit negative emotional reactions that will generalize to the teacher, the classroom, or the subject matter itself.

When applying any of the reduction procedures, keep these rules in mind:

1. Be firm, but stay calm (use a low, steady voice). If you begin to lose control, walk away until you calm down.
2. Respond as soon as possible to a particular act.
3. Be consistent. Say what you mean and mean what you say. Don't threaten and not follow through.
4. Save your feelings for later. Don't say how the misbehavior makes you feel ("You're driving me crazy").
5. Avoid overreacting. Usually small rewards and punishers, when part of a good plan, will work fine.
6. Whenever punishment is used, try to reward an alternative behavior.
7. Above all, direct your criticism at a student's actions, not at the student personally. Hostile questions like "What's wrong with you?" and "Can't you do anything right?" do not get at specific action and should be avoided. (Sparzo, 1985, pp. 42–43).

The following discussion presents twelve strategies for reducing undesirable behaviors.

1. *Instruction.* As indicated in the previous section, one form of instruction involves telling a student what he or she is expected to do. In the case of reducing an undesirable behavior, simply telling some students to stop doing something will work just fine: "Please stop talking, Mary" or "Richard, that's enough of that!" But as teachers know, stronger action is sometimes required.
2. *Situational Changes.* As discussed earlier, the classroom situation itself can exert a powerful influence on student performance. Teachers can also reduce student behaviors by making situational changes, as these examples illustrate:

    - A teacher changed the seat assignments of two students who talked constantly before the change.
    - Jonathan creates fewer disturbances since he was reassigned to Mr. Marshall's class.
    - The amount of junk food eaten by students during school hours has diminished significantly since the vending machines have been removed.
    - School officials have discovered that cleaning up immediately after an act of vandalism seems to suppress vandalism in their school.
    - Ms. McKinney has learned that students make fewer errors when she sits in the middle of a circle of students rather than in front of them.
    - There is less fighting, stealing, and wandering since the local high school hired an off-duty policeman.
    - Students have learned to talk softly during lunch because a light flashes when it gets too noisy.

3. *Differential Reinforcement of Other Behavior (DRO).* DRO is a procedure whereby a reinforcer is delivered at the end of an interval of time during which a misbehavior (target behavior) is absent. Care must be taken not to reinforce other misbehavior (misbehavior other than the target behavior) if it occurs near the end of the specified interval of time. If the target misbehavior does occur during the interval, reinforcement is withheld and a new interval begins. An example will clarify this relatively simple procedure. Suppose a student's average rate of swearing during baseline is once every 10 minutes. In order to set an attainable goal and make reinforcement likely, you set the initial interval at 5 or 10 minutes. If no instances of swearing occur at the end of the interval, you reinforce immediately, say, with praise or points, and begin a new interval. If swearing occurs during the next interval, you withhold reinforcement and move on to a new interval. DRO has been quite effective in reducing many behaviors, including self-injury and hyperactivity, fighting, destructiveness, talkouts, thumbsucking, and soiling oneself. It can be combined rather well with other reductive techniques. For

example, when misbehavior occurs during an interval, a student might lose earned points, and a new interval would begin. Remember these two important points when using DRO: (1) Make the initial interval short enough to insure success; somewhere around the average baseline performance may be a good place to start, and (2) gradually increase the size of the interval as progress is evidenced.

4. *Differential Reinforcement of Incompatible Behavior (DRI).* Rather than reinforce the *absence* of misbehavior, reinforcement can be provided for acts that are functionally incompatible with misbehavior. By *incompatible* we mean that two behaviors cannot occur at the same time. Walking about the room and working at one's desk are incompatible behaviors. Suppose a very active student exhibits several undesirable behaviors such as walking about the room, tapping others on the head, taking things from peers, interrupting others at their desks, and so on. A DRO procedure might be implemented, but the student would probably lose many opportunities for reinforcement since her overactivity would likely result in undesirable behavior during the specified intervals. Consequently, few rewards would be given. DRI is especially appropriate in cases like this when one or more responses need to be reduced. A teacher could select one or two behaviors to reinforce that are incompatible with one or more of the undesirable behaviors. In the case of the overactive child, reinforcement for staying in her seat and working on tasks should do the trick. These two behaviors are incompatible with walking about the room, tapping heads, taking materials, and interrupting others. If you employ a DRI strategy, guard against rewarding socially invalid (unuseful) behaviors.
5. *Differential Reinforcement of Low Rates of Responding (DRL).* DRL is a reinforcement procedure for reducing but not necessarily eliminating a behavior. This strategy is appropriate when a behavior is undesirable only because there is too much of it. Examples of behaviors that should be reduced but not eliminated include unnecessary requests for restroom breaks, excessive questioning, and dominating classroom discussion. By way of illustration, a DRL procedure could be applied in a situation in which a student, Jill, dominates discussions. With a good definition at hand and opting for frequency rather than momentary time sampling recording, we observe the number of comments Jill makes during discussions. Say that she averages 12 comments per minute during baseline. Starting with this average rate, we reward Jill with praise, free time, and opportunities to assist her teacher each time her rate of participation is 12 per minute or below during discussions. Once we have discussed the intervention plan with her, we would inform her about her rate after each discussion session. We would subsequently change requirements for reinforcement until Jill's level of participation fell within a more acceptable range. Several variations of DRL are available. The procedure is generally quite effective, and it can be combined with other strategies for reducing behavior. It is important to use baseline information as a guide for setting reinforcement criteria and for gradually reducing performance.

6. *Extinction.* Extinction is a procedure in which we withhold the reinforcement that has maintained a behavior in the past. Assume that a student, Ron, makes wisecracks while you are teaching and that this behavior has been maintained by the attention you have given it in the past. You originally thought Ron's comments were clever, but now things have gotten out of hand. You decide to ignore Ron's comments unless he first raises his hand. Ignoring in this instance means not attending in any way—saying nothing in response to Ron's comments and not looking in his direction. When you begin to ignore the behavior, you can expect Ron to wisecrack even more and perhaps more aggressively. When behavior is ignored in an extinction procedure, it often alternates between responding and pausing ("extinction bursts"). Thus, the behavior may not decrease gradually or steadily. But if one keeps cool in the face of the outbursts and withholds attention consistently, Ron should eventually stop.

   Extinction works quite well when it is combined with positive reinforcement. That is, one should ignore misbehavior as much as possible while rewarding an alternative performance. In Ron's case, the teacher can use the combined strategies by ignoring all instances of wisecracking and recognizing him when he raises his hand and speaks appropriately. In fact, the combined procedures will probably reduce Ron's wisecracking much faster than extinction alone. Combining the strategies amounts to a DRA procedure, which was labeled the premier strategy for changing behavior in the previous section.

   Under proper circumstances, extinction can reduce a wide range of behaviors including self-depreciating comments ("I just can't do it"), showing off, gossiping, verbal abuse, arguing, and complaining. However, several problems are associated with the use of extinction. It is often difficult to get enough people to ignore someone's behavior consistently. And, of course, some behaviors such as hitting and self-injurious behavior should not be ignored. As indicated above, behavior sometimes gets worse before it gets better under an extinction procedure, and aggression is also a possibility. Finally, even after a behavior has been extinguished, it sometimes recurs at a later time ("spontaneous recovery"). But usually the behavior is weaker than it was before extinction took place. Continued application of the extinction procedure should solve the problem.

7. *Response Cost.* Response cost is a procedure whereby a student or group of students loses a previously earned reward or privilege when an undesirable behavior occurs. In Chapter 1 we called this Type 2 punishment (negative punishment). Although both extinction and response cost reduce behavior, extinction does so by withholding a reward after a response, while response cost involves the removal or loss of a reward.

   Response cost is a relatively easy strategy to administer and, because a reward is removed, teachers have an important opportunity to give the reward back contingent on acceptable behavior. When initiating a response cost procedure, consider having the student forfeit only small amounts of the reward. For example, two minutes lost from recess time for each incident of misconduct is generally preferable to taking away recess entirely. One can always deduct more time (e.g., five minutes for each incident) if need be. It is not unusual for response cost to be combined with token or point systems of reinforcement. If a student is earning points for certain performances in the classroom, some of these points can be taken for undesirable behavior. The student, of course, should be made fully aware of any procedure that involves losing points he has earned.

8. *Reprimanding.* Reprimands are statements such as warnings, rebukes, expressions of disapproval, and saying "no" that follow behavior in an effort to reduce or eliminate it ("I've told you a thousand times to stop it, Dane," "Cut it out!"). Reprimands, unlike instruction, come after rather than before an act. Reprimands are quite common in schools and homes, perhaps because they are so easy to use. This strategy is placed arbitrarily near the end of the list of reductive procedures because the line between reprimanding and verbal abuse can be quite thin. Also, because a reprimand is a form of Type 1 punishment (positive punishment), the person who relies on this approach to discipline risks being disliked by students. Reprimands would not have survived centuries of use if they did not work on occasion. However, as teachers know, their use can backfire. Chapter 6 notes that reprimanding students for getting out of their seats can actually increase standing, due, perhaps, to the attention that accompanies the reprimands. If on occasion a reprimand is called for, try to deliver it firmly, quietly, and, if possible, in private. Reprimanding students in front of others may be counterproductive.
9. *Time Out (TO).* Time out is a procedure in which an individual is denied access to the reinforcers in a setting contingent on misconduct. It has been applied in many different settings and, when properly administered, is effective in reducing a variety of behaviors, including hitting, self-injury, noncompliance, tantrums, crying, inappropriate talking (e.g., swearing), and destructiveness. TO is basically a Type 2 punishment procedure. There are two basic forms of TO, nonexclusionary and exclusionary. In nonexclusionary TO, the student remains in the classroom but is kept from participating in various reinforcing activities (talking with others, playing, moving about the classroom) for a specified period of time, usually 2 to 15 minutes. In effect, the person is removed from reinforcement immediately after misbehavior. In exclusionary TO, the student is sent or taken to another place, called a time-out room. This room should be devoid of reinforcement (e.g., no interesting objects to play with), boring, and very safe.

The following outline is one among several versions of time out:

(a) Tell the student about TO and how it will work in his case. If it seems helpful, roleplay the entire procedure with him in private. Let him know what will happen if he refuses to go to TO (consider response cost measures).
(b) Give one warning when the student misbehaves: "Stan, if you do that again, you'll go to TO."
(c) If misconduct continues, lead the student to the TO area, calmly and silently. Ignore complaints. If it seems helpful, tell the student why he is going to TO. Be objective and impersonal. Stay with the facts about the misbehavior ("You can't throw things about the room") and the TO procedure.
(d) If the student is disruptive in the time-out room (yells, makes noise), ignore it.
(e) Permit the student to leave when time is up, usually 2 to 15 minutes, *provided that he is acting appropriately* (not shouting, swearing, and so on). If not, he is to remain in TO for another minute. Behavior should be acceptable for 15 to 30 seconds prior to release. If not, have the student remain for another minute. As before, he is to engage in acceptable behavior for the last 15 to 30 seconds.
(f) Upon his return to the classroom, "catch him being good" and reward him for it.

Although TO has been used quite effectively, several problems might arise as you use it. Some people might object to exclusionary time out on humanitarian grounds, perhaps because they have seen or heard about its misuse. Another potential problem is that some students will simply not go to the TO area. Because of these and other concerns, you should seek professional assistance if you have little or no experience with TO procedures. It is also advisable to secure appropriate adult consent before you intervene with an exclusionary TO procedure.

A convenient nonexclusionary time-out procedure for younger students is worthy of note. This procedure involves constructing a "time for reinforcement" badge to be worn by all students. Students have access to all rewards normally available in the classroom (talking, free time, privileges, play, and so on) while the badge is worn. When disruptive behavior occurs, the student gives up his badge. Surrendering the badge signals the beginning of a short time-out period, at which time the student is not eligible for rewards. When time out is over, the badge is returned to the student, providing his behavior is acceptable during time out. He now has access to rewards once again. Like all time-out procedures, this version is not likely to work if the classroom is unrewarding in the first place.

10. *Overcorrection.* Overcorrection is a Type 1 punishment procedure. It consists of two components, although the second component is more often found in classrooms: (1) restitution and (2) positive practice.

Restitution overcorrection consists of requiring a student to correct, actually overcorrect, the effects of misbehavior. Suppose that a student keeps a messy desk, despite previous attempts to correct the problem. Restitution overcorrection could be applied in this case by requiring the student to clean not only her desk but several others desks as well. Positive practice overcorrection requires a student to practice correct, actually overly correct, forms of an appropriate behavior in the setting in which misconduct usually occurs. Thus, in the previous case, the student might be required to clean her desk repeatedly. Since overcorrection is by definition punishment, no reinforcement should occur while the student is engaged in restitution or positive practice or both.

Overcorrection has been used with mentally retarded children and adults, autistic children, and emotionally disturbed individuals. It has also been used to reduce aggressive and disruptive behaviors, toilet accidents, tantrums, self-injurious behavior, shouting, swearing, out-of-seat behavior, and so on. Because overcorrection requires close supervision to insure that the student engages in the appropriate behaviors (instruction and physical prompting are often required), its use may cause some problems for you. You might have to postpone your use of this strategy to a time that is more convenient for you.

11. *Negative practice.* Negative practice is a technique used to reduce behavior by requiring the person to engage in the misconduct to the point of aversiveness. One mother stopped her daughters from jumping on their beds by requiring them to continue doing so beyond the point of enjoyment. In a school setting, some behaviors, such as throwing paper wads or swearing, might be eliminated similarly, away from the view of others.
12. *Contingent effort.* This procedure involves expending effort contingent on each incident of misconduct. Each time misconduct occurs, the student is instructed to expend effort, say, by sitting on the floor and standing up several times (5, 10, 15 times) in rapid succession. The procedure should be done in private. It would be wise to secure consent from appropriate adults before using this punishment procedure.

This chapter touched on some useful procedures for modifying social and academic behaviors. Its emphasis has been on individual behavior. However, several of the strategies—for example, point systems and response cost procedures—can be applied in group settings. The final section of this chapter illustrates this point.

For some time, Mr. Taylor has been concerned about the amount of time he spends nagging his ninth-grade students to follow classroom rules. He has tried special privileges, threats, and reprimands. Nothing seems to work. Realizing that a more systematic plan is needed, he has implemented the following nine-step plan introduced in Chapter 1.

STEPS	DESCRIPTION
1. Define behavior	• In-seat: Bottom touching sitting surface of assigned seat. • On-task: Appropriate engagement in assigned work. • Talking: Only with permission.
2. Observe and record	• Momentary time sampling: Varying number of students out-of-seat, off-task, talking throughout the day.
3. Set attainable goal	• All students follow classroom rules.
4. Identify rewards	• Students especially like word games and computers (activity rewards).
5. Select strategies	• Students given 20 minutes free time for access to word games and computer at end of day. • Numbers 20 to 0 minutes placed on chalkboard. • Timer set to sound at unpredictable intervals. If anyone is violating a rule when timer sounds, the top-most number is erased from the chalkboard. Thus, students lose one minute for each infraction (response cost).
6. Rehearse procedures	• Rules clarified (instruction). Dry run implemented.
7. Implement plan	• Done after rehearsing the plan.
8. Monitor results	• Time sampling done intermittently. Teacher and students pleased with results.
9. Maintain gains	• Point system gradually eliminated (fading). • Praise continued. • Other activity rewards made available.

Another illustration of a group procedure is called the *Good Behavior Game*, which combines several strategies and is useful for either increasing or decreasing behaviors. It has three main features: (1) specification of behaviors, (2) posted feedback, and (3) reinforcement based on the comparative performance of two (or more) groups of students.

Students are first assigned to one of two groups. The behaviors to be changed are then explained and posted on the chalkboard. When the target behavior occurs (e.g., answering a question), it is posted under the team's name on the chalkboard whose member answered the question.

Reinforcement for appropriate performance is given to the team if a predetermined and posted standard is reached or exceeded. If both teams reach or exceed the standard, both receive reinforcement. If neither team reaches criterion, neither team wins. However, the team having the highest total may receive the reward. The Good Behavior Game can be used to increase a variety of desirable behaviors, such as homework completion, being on time, and so on.

The procedure is also useful for reducing behaviors. Reinforcement for appropriate performance is given to the team that does not exceed a predetermined standard. For example, if a team does not exceed three incidents of quarreling per day, it receives reinforcement. If both teams fall below the posted criterion, both teams are declared winners. If the standard is exceeded by both teams, the team with the lowest total may get the reward or part of the reward.

Suppose, for example, a teacher wanted to reduce hitting, noncompliance, out-of-seat, and stealing. After explaining the behaviors to his students (clear definitions will help) and posting a maximum standard for the behaviors, he might determine the cumulative total for each team for all behaviors. The team whose total stays below a standard wins, unless the other team also remains below the standard. In this case, both teams are proclaimed winners.

SELF-QUIZ

In the column on the right, write in a corrective strategy that fits the descriptive statement given in the left column.

DESCRIPTION	STRATEGY
1. A student lost a minute of recess for each minute he came late to class.	____________
2. A student, his teacher, and his parents have specified in writing the relationship between homework assignments and access to privileges at home.	____________
3. "The result of this operation is then inserted into the equation."	____________
4. Toby repeatedly apologized to his teacher and classmates for throwing paper wads around the room.	____________
5. Toby was required to pick up the paper wads he threw plus all other classroom objects not in their proper place.	____________

6. Doris earned a point toward free-time opportunities each time she went 15 minutes without criticizing others. ____________

7. By paying attention to their teacher's gestures, students have learned when to answer "yes" or "no" to her questions. ____________

8. A teacher underlined the words in a reading passage that she wanted her students to pay close attention to. ____________

9. Joan discovered that she does homework more quickly before rather than after school hours. She's adjusted her schedule accordingly. ____________

10. Leslie swears only when he is around Bob, who "swears like a trooper." ____________

11. A teacher lost weight because he ate only special sack lunches prepared by his wife. ____________

12. Butch has to sit in a boring part of the classroom each time he annoys others. ____________

13. A teacher continued using expressions of approval for good student performance, while gradually eliminating the use of points. ____________

14. A teacher no longer pays attention to Mack's whining. ____________

15. A teacher acknowledges students if they raise their hands before talking and ignores those who do not. ____________

16. Ms. Pauly said, "Jim, you'll have to wait until Frances finishes before you talk." ____________

17. Mr. Jamal is teaching Sal a new behavior by rewarding Sal's step-by-step progression to the new behavior. ____________

Solutions

(1) Deducting time from recess contingent on lateness is a response cost procedure (Type 2 punishment). (2) A home-based contract has been negotiated. (3) It is reasonable to assume that this statement serves as instruction. (4) & (5) Because Toby was required to repeatedly practice an appropriate act, positive practice overcorrection was applied in situation 4 and restitution overcorrection in the next episode. When someone can improve the environment to a condition better than it was before misconduct, both forms of overcorrection may be appropriate, as in situations 4 and 5. (6) DRO is illustrated in Doris's case. (7) The teacher has provided questionable prompting because gestures drew students' attention away from the questions themselves. (8) This situation illustrates appropriate prompting because underlining key words focuses student attention on critical stimuli. (9) Changing the time when she does homework has been an important situational change for Joan. (10) Leslie may be imitating Bob, whose swearing serves as a model for Leslie. (11) A change in the situation, sack lunches, has helped the teacher lose weight. (12) Butch is in nonexclusionary time out. (13) The teacher has faded an artificial or contrived technique (points) in favor of more natural social reinforcement. (14) Extinction (ignoring) is illustrated in this episode. (15) The teacher has positively reinforced alternative performance (DRA). (16) Ms. Pauly has given a directive (instruction), assuming that her comment was made before Jim spoke. (17) Mr. Jamal is using successive approximation (shaping).

CHAPTER 5 / REHEARSING, IMPLEMENTING, MONITORING, AND MAINTAINING

This chapter provides a description of the final four steps of the general plan for behavior change first presented in Chapter 1. Even though the chapter is brief, its topic, nonetheless, is quite important. It would be very disappointing, for example, to work hard to improve student performance only to see performance return to its former level when intervention is withdrawn. In such a case, the behavior change plan has broken down at step 9 (maintenance). The goal of a sound behavior change program should be not only improved performance but the maintenance and generalization (transfer) of that performance across appropriate settings as well.

REHEARSING

People often learn more quickly if they are shown as well as told what to do. Step 6 in the behavior change plan calls for practicing or roleplaying key elements of an intervention procedure. You might consider, for example, demonstrating what arguing means to a student as well as others who will be involved in your plan, practicing a time-out procedure in private before implementation, or showing parents how to record mock data in a home-based contract procedure. Rehearsing or roleplaying key elements of an intervention plan enables participants to experience conditions very much like those they will experience when the plan is put into effect. A key advantage to rehearsal is that immediate feedback can be provided after action. Such feedback is less likely when people are merely told what to do.

IMPLEMENTING

Before you apply a behavior change strategy, check to see that the student clearly understands what is expected of her (rehearsal may help), that others who will be involved are fully apprised of your plan and their role in it (rehearsal may help), and that procedures will be applied consistently. It is important to realize that other people involved in intervention (parents, other teachers, the principal, the school nurse) can make or break your plan. So select team members with care.

MONITORING

Monitoring calls for observing the target behavior using the same methods of observation used to gather baseline information. Comparing information from this phase of the plan with baseline information will allow you to judge what effect, if any, intervention is having on the target behavior. Use the results of this comparison to make needed changes in your plan. For example, if you find that progress is being slowed by a flaw in a negotiated contract, present this information to those involved in the contract. One possibility is that promised rewards are not being delivered as scheduled in the contract. Those involved in the contract should act on this information.

Do not expect immediate improvements. In fact, the target behavior may get worse before it gets better during the first days of intervention. Do not change your plan until you are reasonably certain why it isn't working. Seek answers to questions like: Is the behavior clearly specified? Are key people cooperating? Are initial standards for reinforcement too high? Is the student motivated? If not, why not? Is the size of the rewards too small? Might other things function as rewards? Have the suggestions for selecting and using rewards been incorporated into the plan (see pages 30–31)? Is the plan being applied consistently?

MAINTAINING

Once new behavior has been acquired, steps must be taken to assure that it will be maintained (retained) and that it will generalize (transfer) to new settings. This is a very important aspect of all teaching. Many learned behaviors are neither retained nor used when students leave school. Because many otherwise good behavior change programs break down at this point in the process, the following procedures are highly recommended.

1. *Apply effective procedures in different settings.* If DRO, for example, reduces swearing in your classroom for a period of time (maintenance), consider recommending it to other teachers who may be troubled by the students' swearing. If DRO also reduces swearing in their classrooms, generalization has occurred across settings.
2. *Train loosely.* Procedures that are rigidly applied may inhibit generalization. Thus, you should try to use strategies in flexible ways when you can. For instance, rather than apply an intervention procedure only during morning hours, apply it on occasion at other times of the day as well. Flexibility might also be introduced by using more than one strategy, or by assigning a colleague or classmate of the student a role in implementation.
3. *Program common elements.* Program elements in your strategic plan that are common to your classroom and to other settings as well. For example, rather than permit students to claim backup rewards twice each

day (in a token system), reinforcement delays can be introduced by scheduling exchanges at the end of the day, then after two days, three days, and so on. Here the common element is the delays, because in everyday life the student will experience many delays in reinforcement.

4. *Use a variety of antecedent stimuli.* Requiring students to respond to a variety of stimuli before they act is likely to promote generalization. As an example, assume that you want to teach a student to initiate conversation, and that you are using roleplaying to do so. If you were to follow the advice given here, you would have the student roleplay not only with you but with others as well. You might also vary the theme of each roleplaying episode as you proceed.
5. *Gradually eliminate (fade) artificial rewards and procedures.* A major goal of good programming is to maintain behavior change with natural consequences (such as smiles and praise, which normally follow behavior) rather than artificial ones (points, tokens). This can be accomplished by gradually eliminating artificial or contrived rewards or procedures at the same time the individual is exposed to natural events. Actually, the use of artificial procedures can make natural procedures even more effective. For example, if a friendly teacher uses smiles and praise along with points to reward academic performance, her smiles and other expressions of approval could become even more influential due to their association with the points that are being used.

SELF-QUIZ

Determine whether rehearsing, implementing, monitoring, or maintaining (generalization) is the major theme in the episodes below. Write your answer in the space provided after each episode.

EPISODES	ANSWER
1. Mr. Rosenberg's student teacher recorded David's chair tipping for one week prior to intervention. The student teacher continued to record during intervention. A graph of the data indicated no reduction in chair tipping until the third day of intervention.	______________
2. To help Lois overcome her shyness in meeting people, Mr. Cosby wrote out specific words Lois was to say to initiate conversations. He spent five minutes each day with Lois, during which Lois read the words and Mr. Cosby roleplayed the new person.	______________

3. Ms. Nall was pleased with Pat's progress in beginning his work and not dawdling. She asked Pat's chemistry teacher to praise the same target behavior during chemistry class for two weeks. She then gradually reduced the amount of praise she gave. ______________________

4. Jan likes to make stuffed dolls out of her mother's old nylon stockings. Her teacher, Mrs. Spencer, solicited cooperation from Jan's mother, who promised to let Jan work on her dolls only when Mrs. Spencer would send a note home saying that Jan had earned 10 points for not talking out during class. Jan agreed to the arrangement. ______________________

Solutions

(1) The student teacher observed and monitored David's chair tipping both during baseline and intervention. (2) Mr. Cosby used rehearsal (roleplaying) to help Lois practice what to say to new people. (3) By asking the chemistry teacher to praise Pat for getting down to work quickly, Ms. Nall was hoping that the target behavior would be maintained and generalize to other classroom settings. (4) Jan's mother was helping implement a behavior change plan by providing a favorite activity at home.

REFLECTIONS

1. It is interesting to discover what reinforcers and punishers affect our own behaviors. Keep a personal journal for a day in which you note incidents of reinforcement and punishment in your daily life. Did you count more reinforcements or more punishments? What did you find especially rewarding? What was your most disturbing punishment?
2. A teacher claims that one of her students doesn't complete assignments because "he's just plain lazy." Given the discussion about defining behavior in Chapter 2, what is wrong with this explanation of behavior? Write a more plausible explanation.
3. Some people believe that changing behavior by the deliberate use of reinforcers is a form of bribery. Given the broad range of consequent events that affect our lives, do you agree? Why or why not?
4. Punishment can elicit negative emotional reactions that linger well beyond the punishing incident itself. Think of other disadvantages of punishment. Jot these down and share them with someone in a discussion.
5. This text suggests that desirable behaviors be reinforced when punishment is used. Suggest some alternative behaviors to be rewarded for each of the following: arguing, destructiveness, name calling, tattling, and thumbsucking.
6. It is necessary to know about the target behavior prior to any implementation of a behavior change plan. Discuss the importance of baseline information when deciding what behavior to reward at the beginning of an intervention program.
7. People watching is a favorite pastime for many people. Visit a classroom, cafeteria, library, playground, shopping mall, or any other place of interest. Select a behavior to define, record, and graph. Share your results with others.
8. Teachers who do not understand the importance of reinforcement in changing behavior seem to rely on a negative approach in their instruction. Assign someone the role of a teacher who is attempting to justify his use of reprimands, exclusionary time out, and corporal punishment as a means to discipline students. Assign others the following roles: a student who has been punished by the teacher, a classmate, and the punished student's parents. Ask the participants to discuss the disciplinary methods of the teacher from the perspective of the roles they are playing.
9. One simple method to bring about behavior change is the use of prompts. Sometimes, that is all that is needed. List possible prompts for teaching a social or academic behavior and suggest ways to fade the prompts.
10. Some students seem to learn more quickly when they can see an example as well as hear the instructions. How might you combine instruction and modeling to teach a student to initiate conversation? How might you combine the strategies to teach an academic performance?
11. One goal of good instruction is to have students use newly learned skills in environments other than where the skills were learned. Assume that you have taught someone to initiate conversation with you. How might you proceed to encourage the behavior in other settings?

12. Students can apply the nine-step plan to their own behaviors in a self-management (self-control) program. Discuss some of the ways the plan could be used to improve study behaviors or other behaviors of interest.
13. Read one or more of the references listed below and compare the discussions with those in this book. At the end of Part II, references that focus on specific behavioral strategies (for instance, maintaining behavior, contracting, time out) should be especially helpful.

Alberto, P. A., & Troutman, A. C. (1985). *Applied behavior analysis for teachers* (2nd ed.). Columbus, OH: Charles E. Merrill.

Baldwin, J. D., & Baldwin, J. I. (1986). *Behavior principles in everyday life* (2nd ed.). Englewood Cliffs, NJ: Prentice-Hall.

Becker, W. C. (1986). *Applied psychology for teachers: A behavioral cognitive approach.* Chicago: SRA.

Bellack, A. S., & Hersen, M. (Eds.). (1985). *Dictionary of behavior therapy techniques.* New York: Pergamon Press.

Evans, W. H., Evans, S. S., & Schmid, R. E. (1989). *Behavior and instructional management.* Boston: Allyn & Bacon.

Cooper, J. P., Heron, T. E., & Heward, W. L. (1987). *Applied behavior analysis.* Columbus, OH: Charles E. Merrill.

Sparzo, F. J. (1985). *Changing behavior: A practical guide for teachers and parents.* Bloomington, IN: Phi Delta Kappa Educational Foundation.

Sulzer-Azaroff, B., & Mayer, G. R. (1986). *Achieving educational excellence using behavioral strategies.* New York: Holt, Rinehart and Winston.

PART II

SPECIFIC BEHAVIOR PROBLEMS

Part II consists of 36 specific behavior problems that all regular and special education teachers face from time to time. Each problem has been placed in one of nine chapters according to broad descriptions of related behaviors. Chapters 6 through 14 cover problems associated with school or academic tasks, verbal behavior, aggressive acts, dishonesty, social interaction, immaturity, sense of self, body and personal habits, and, finally, special populations. Placement of problems in a particular chapter has been arbitrary for the most part. For example, although cheating, lying, and stealing are subsumed under the general topic of dishonesty in Chapter 9, they could have been placed in Chapter 10 (problems related to social interaction) or Chapter 11 (problems related to immaturity).

The discussion of each specific behavior begins with a list of DETECTION behaviors, or actions commonly associated with a target behavior. Thus, because students who cheat on examinations sometimes use "crib notes," the use of such notes is identified as one possible indicator of cheating. To return to a point made earlier, what constitutes too much behavior (e.g., inattention, off-task, out-of-seat) or too little (e.g., motivation, participation, self-esteem) requires informed judgment by the teacher or other professional. He or she must judge what is appropriate and inappropriate behavior in a particular classroom.

The discussion moves on to a *Description* of the target behavior, one that, along with the list of possible actions, may help you formulate a working definition of the behavior as you observe a particular student in a particular setting. Next, some *Implications* or problems associated with each target behavior are mentioned. The implications are based more on interpretation and logical prediction than on empirical research. To illustrate this point, the student who acts dishonestly risks being shunned by others, while one who is constantly away from his seat will probably learn less than he should.

The next section, *Controlling Factors*, focuses on the antecedent or A events of behavior discussed in Chapter 1. Here we can only suggest what some of the controlling (antecedent) factors might be for the target behaviors discussed. Whenever you can identify the events that trigger a behavior (this is often very difficult to do), try to incorporate them in your plan of action in some way. Suppose, for example, you discover that two students who talk incessantly do so when they sit together but not otherwise. The immediate controlling factor might simply be the seating arrangement for these students. In this case, you might separate the students and acknowledge them in some way as their rate of talking diminishes. Consequent (C) events are also identified in this section. The final section for each problem lists intervention procedures for correcting (changing) performance.

The CORRECTION procedures listed for each problem are presented in an order that reflects a general preference for reinforcement over aversive procedures. No claim is made that all the interventions listed for each problem have been tested and found to work for that problem. In most cases, the research is still too fragmented to make such a claim. When selecting procedures to use with a student, start with those listed first and work your way down the list, if necessary. Be prepared to adapt the interventions you select to your particular circumstances. *Combine strategies when it makes good sense to do so.* As an illustration, instruction is often combined with modeling and various forms of attention and approval, while time out is sometimes combined with a response cost procedure. But regardless of the procedures used, always acknowledge gains in student performance with various forms of attention and approval.

The nine chapters in Part II focus on detecting and correcting a wide range of specific behavior problems confronting teachers. Each problem provides *background information* as you apply the nine-step plan for behavior change presented in Part I. For instance, should you be concerned with a student who acts impulsively, the information found in Chapter 7 may help you define *impulsivity* (step 1 of the general plan) as well as select appropriate procedures for reducing it (step 5). The "Reflections" section at the close of Part II may help you to think about and interpret your new knowledge.

1. IMPULSIVENESS

DETECTION Watch for these behaviors.

- Student responds instantly with little or no hesitation
- Student makes frequent errors, apparently from lack of planning
- Student responds before instructions are completed
- Student is intolerant of delays in receiving feedback

Description. Impulsiveness involves acting before thinking with little or no anticipation of possible alternative responses. Responses are often immediate or instant (frequently shifting from one thing to another; difficulty in waiting one's turn) and lead to errors.

Implications. Impulsiveness is the opposite of reflective behavior in which the student takes time to deliberate before responding. It should be differentiated from responses given by students who make immediate but correct responses. Impulsiveness is highly correlated with inattention (see Problem 2) and overactivity (see Problem 27). Responses made by impulsive students may be incorrect perhaps because little time is spent thinking about an answer. Impulsive behavior can interfere with acceptance by peers who may view the student as rude or ill-mannered. Students who respond too quickly may experience difficulty sharing or participating in give-and-take communication with others (see Problem 12—Interrupting). Also, because many responses are incorrect, those who act impulsively may earn lower grades than they would if they responded with more deliberation.

Controlling Factors. Although some forms of impulsiveness are associated with learning disabilities that are said to be based in central nervous system dysfunctioning, most forms of impulsiveness may be viewed in terms of the inability to tolerate delays in feedback or reinforcement. The general strategy for change involves teaching the student to delay responding while considering alternative solutions to a problem.

CORRECTION Try one or more of these procedures.

1. *Instruction and Modeling.* Talk with the student in private. Explain what *impulsive* means, emphasizing the difference, with examples, between impulsive and reflective or deliberate thought. Model slow and careful problem solving and reward the student's attempts at imitation.
2. *Situational Changes.* Consider making the following situational changes:
    a. Place the student in situations where there are few distractions.
    b. Provide a series of short tasks (5 to 10 minutes each) that require accuracy and thoughtful action, not speed.
    c. Separate the student from other students (and adults) who respond impulsively, at least during those times when the student needs to concentrate on tasks.
3. *Self-Instruction.* Teach the student reflective self-instruction. If possible, provide a different task each day as you take the student through the following procedure:
    a. Talk aloud as you solve a problem in front of the student ("Let's see. What do I do first? First, I will need to determine what kind of problem this is. It's an addition problem. It has 4 columns of 4-digit numbers to be added. Next, I'll need to add this column of numbers. That's 28. Next, I'll have to ..."). At this point, you are modeling reflective self-instruction.
    b. Ask the student to solve the same problem while you direct him aloud in the manner you directed yourself in the previous step. This is instruction on your part and imitation on the student's part.
    c. The student then solves the problem, talking aloud to himself. This is overt self-instruction.
    d. The problem is solved once again by the student but in a whisper. Overt self-instruction is being faded.
    e. The student solves the problem a final time and talks to himself privately. This is covert self-instruction. At this point, encourage the student to go beyond the self-talk you have modeled. Suggest that he invent his own self-instruction, such as "Slow down. I'd better think of 2 or 3 possibilities before I answer."
    f. Suggest that the student reward himself for solving the problem. He could, for example, think something positive about himself ("I'm getting good at that"), or engage in some other pleasant thought.

As a variation of this procedure consider using a technique called "Stop, Look, Listen, Act." The teacher might compare this procedure to what the driver of a car does when arriving at a railroad crossing. The driver stops the car, looks and listens, determines that it is safe to continue, and then drives on. The use of a traffic-signal drawing or circles to represent the colored lights can provide prompts to the following steps in the game:

RED light means:	Stop
YELLOW light means:	Look, Listen, and determine an appropri ate response
GREEN light means:	Act

If it seems appropriate, have the student draw the stoplight on a card as a prompt and tape it to his desk so that it is in full view at all times. Be sure to model the the use of this game for the student and have the student imitate your procedures.

4. *Help Student Focus on Differences.* Impulsive students may focus on the features of a new problem that are like the features of problems with which they are familiar. Consider, for example, squares and rectangles. Both figures share 3 common features: 4 sides, straight sides, and 90-degree angles. The figures differ in that only opposite sides of rectangles are equal. If the difference in the length of sides is small in a rectangle, we would predict more difficulty in discriminating a square from a rectangle than if the difference in the length of the sides is large. Directing the student's attention to differences in the features of new and familiar problems is likely to reduce the number of errors made.
5. *Delays in Responding.* Ask the student to delay responding to tasks for a specific amount of time. If necessary, consider letting him earn points for evidence of deliberation, such as a written list of several alternative responses to a given problem. Points can be exchanged for attractive backup reinforcers.
6. *Peer Imitation.* Let the student work with a "deliberate thinker." Ask both students to identify several alternative responses for each task. For example, ask the students to solve problems in mathematics in more than 1 way, to provide a specified number of synonyms and antonyms for each word on a list, to give several examples of a concept or principle, or to rewrite a paragraph several different ways without changing its essential meaning. When possible, ask the students to rank the alternative responses to each task from best to worst. When "best" answers occurred after other alternatives were identified, call this to the attention of the students. The point is, of course, that impulsive or first answers are sometimes not the best ones.

7. *Praise Reflective Thinking.* When you observe the student responding with deliberation, acknowledge it in some way. The reward can be in the form of praise, such as "You thought before you answered (or acted). That's great!" or "Nice going. You stopped, looked, and listened before you acted."
8. *Ignore Impulsive Behaviors.* When the student responds impulsively, ignore the student's response and acknowledge other students who respond more appropriately. Point out why other students have been recognized. For example, you might say, "I'm calling on you, Jill, because you thought about the answer before you raised your hand."
9. *Reassign Tasks.* Ask students to redo assignments if they show signs of impulsive action.
10. *Response Cost.* Devise a response cost procedure for errors. If you employ response cost, provide plenty of rewards for correct responses. See the discussion concerning response cost in Chapter 4. For instance, you might give the student a certain number of points at the beginning of the plan. When impulsive behavior is noted, the student loses a point. The remaining points are exchanged for prespecified backup reinforcers.

- *Additional Suggestions.* Consider rewarding students for (a) written or oral reports describing how they used reflective self-instruction or self-control successfully, (b) calling your attention to incidents in which peers or adults (including you) considered alternatives before acting, or (c) teaching the self-instruction technique described in Procedure 3 to other students.

2. INATTENTION

DETECTION Watch for these behaviors.

- Student's body orientation and eyes are frequently directed away from instructional stimuli or events
- Student often talks or behaves inappropriately during instruction
- Student is often unaware of the question that has been asked
- Student is easily distracted

Description. Lack of attention is one of the most frequent complaints teachers have about students. It is nearly impossible to be absolutely certain that students are not paying attention. For example, a student can be wandering about the room, looking at a book, or tying her shoes while maintaining attention to classroom tasks. Nevertheless, it is quite likely that a student is inattentive when engaging in behaviors incompatible with the task at hand. For example, it is almost impossible to fully attend to what one is reading while talking with a neighbor. Inattention, then, is not focusing directly on a task or activity. The term *Attention Deficit Disorder (ADD)* is frequently used to describe students who are inattentive, impulsive, and hyperactive. (See related Problems 1—Impulsiveness and 26—Overactivity.)

Implications. Inattention can result in incorrect and incomplete work. If inattention is persistent, academic failure is sure to follow and possibly lowered self-esteem as well.

Controlling Factors. A student attends to certain stimuli or events because she has been reinforced for doing so. When a student interacts with classroom activities and materials in reinforcing ways, the activities and materials become interesting and meaningful to her. It is the responsibility of the teacher to direct the student's attention to appropriate stimuli and events: chalkboard, visual displays, reciting person, task, and so on. Once attending is assured, it should be rewarded. Sometimes our daydreaming or private thoughts are more rewarding and compelling than paying attention to the academic tasks of the classroom.

CORRECTION Try one or more of these procedures.

1. *Private Talk.* If inattention is a recurring concern, discuss the matter with the student privately. Hidden factors may be operating unknown to the teacher. (See the discussion on hidden influences in Chapter 1.) Let the student know you are concerned about her inattention and solicit information that can contribute to your understanding of the problem.
2. *Use Instructions and Prompts.* There are many ways to control the student's attention visually and auditorily. Proximity and gently touching the student are both powerful attention controllers. When working at the chalkboard, tap the chalk on the chalkboard; while looking at the student, say something like "Everyone look at this." When giving verbal instructions, interrupt your directions with a comment such as "And the next step is particularly important" or "Listen carefully to what I am going to say next." Use a change in voice tone and volume or make an obviously long pause before saying a special word to emphasize particularly important points. When giving instructions, make one of the steps inappropriate or humorous, and praise the first student who notices it. Make the important visual letter, word, or instruction stand out from the others by using colored chalk, larger print, and so on. Use plenty of praise when students respond appropriately to your efforts.
3. *Use the Student's Name.* When it is obvious that the student is not paying attention, ask, "Amy, are you paying attention?" or say, "Patty, it is important that you get these directions correct." In a more indirect way, use the student's name in an example you are presenting. Students who hear their own names suddenly pay attention.
4. *Remove Distractions.* Remove all stimuli that distract the student. If materials, such as crayons, are on her desk, keep the crayons in your desk and make them available contingent upon the student's attention to the proper tasks. Seat the student in a study carrel or place her desk away from windows, facing a blank wall. Listening to quiet music on a personal headset may block out distractions for some students.

- *Additional Suggestions.* Have the student sit beside others who have learned to pay close attention to tasks. Do all you can to increase the student's rate of task completion. Completing more tasks will automatically increase student attention.

3. NONCOMPLETION OF TASKS

DETECTION Watch for these behaviors.

- Student turns in incomplete work
- Student begins but rarely completes assignments

Description. Noncompletion of tasks is observed when a student begins tasks but does not finish them.

Implications. Persistent noncompletion of tasks is associated with low academic achievement.

Controlling Factors. Tasks are left incomplete when the student finds other activities more rewarding, when the student seeks to avoid an evaluation of her work, or when assigned tasks are inappropriate for the student's age, grade, and ability. Poorly designed and improperly assigned teaching materials are a major source of frustration for some students.

CORRECTION Try one or more of these procedures.

1. *Private Talk.* Try to understand the problem from the student's perspective. What reasons does she give for noncompletion? Are there special difficulties at home or school that you should know about? For example, she may feel pressured by time, or she may not understand a task. If understanding is a problem, have the student restate and explain the directions as well as describe how she will go about completing the task. Clarify any misunderstandings.
2. *Instruction.* Provide remedial instruction if prerequisite skills are lacking. If necessary, consider making alternative assignments. Provide plenty of attention and other rewards as the student begins to complete assigned tasks.
3. *Reassign Incomplete Work.* When work is incomplete, reassign it as homework that is due the next day or within some reasonable period of time. This can be a critical strategy.
4. *Successive Approximations.* For students who consistently do not complete assignments, break the assigned tasks into smaller parts and reward the completion of each of these (reinforcement of successive approximations). Gradually make each part a larger section of the total assignment until only 1 assignment is made and completed.
5. *Premack Principle.* Review the discussion of the Premack Principle in Chapter 3. Make various reinforcing activities available upon completion of work. Some of these activities may be determined by observing the student. Note those activities the student frequently engages in and select appropriate ones as reinforcers. For example, you might say, "When you finish your work, you may have 10 minutes to quietly talk with Kelly" or "You may go to recess when your work is completed."

6. *Contracts.* Write a contract with the student that specifies rewards available upon work completion. You might want to contact the parents for their support. Ask them to permit privileges at home only when work is completed. You will have to keep them informed. Sending appropriate information home with the student has worked well in some cases.
7. *Response Cost.* If work is not completed by the due date at school, remove a privilege. For example, the student will not be permitted to engage in some favored social activity. An alternative is to lower the student's grade by a small amount for each day the work is late, *if you are sure that the student has the prerequisite skills to perform the task.*

- *Additional Suggestions.* Be sure to give verbal praise or other rewards when work is turned in on time and assignments are complete.

4. NONCOMPLIANCE

DETECTION Watch for these behaviors.

- Student ignores requests
- Student does not follow classroom rules
- Student may be argumentative
- Student engages in competitive rather than cooperative action

Description. Noncompliance is deliberate disobedience of requests made by teachers and others. The noncompliant student may be competitive in a negative sense and "have a mind of his own." Teachers may say, "I don't know what I'm going to do with that boy; he never does what he's told." The student may become angry and frustrated at having to do what is requested.

Implications. The persistently noncompliant student is seldom liked by his teacher or peers. He is frequently at odds with others. His behavior demands attention because of its rebellious, nonconforming, and often disruptive nature. Students may sense the teacher's negative feelings and adopt them as their own. Consequently, the noncompliant student may be socially rejected. His friends are likely to be associates who share and value noncompliant behaviors. (See related Problems 6—Talking without Permission, 10—Unsatisfactory Homework, 12—Interrupting, and 23—Attention Seeking.

Controlling Factors. Noncompliant behaviors are learned because they have been reinforced. In fact, even nonverbal negative reactions to the noncompliant behavior may function as reinforcement for noncompliance. The student may feel a sense of control over others by causing them unhappiness or disrupting their lives in some way. Noncompliant behavior can also be learned from role models in the family or from associates. In the classroom, these rewards (hidden reinforcers) may not be apparent.

CORRECTION Try one or more of these procedures.

1. *Private Talk.* Talk with the student privately. Attempt to determine if requests are ignored because of skill deficits or for some other reason. Try to uncover what controlling factors might be operating. Let the student know that he must comply with classroom rules and requests along with other students. Point out acceptable ways in which the student can question rules and requests. Stress the educational and social purposes of your requests. It is important to look at the problem in terms of inappropriate learning rather than in personal terms ("You've been a disobedient kid for a long time").

2. *Instruction and Situational Changes.* Tell the student to do what is requested when he is noncompliant. You might say something like, "Please do what I asked, Billy." Make sure that he has all necessary materials, such as books, dictionaries, paper, and so on. If a particular book is required, place it on or near his desk. A word of caution is in order: In addition to your attention to the noncompliant behavior, be certain that you give attention and praise to a variety of appropriate behaviors. Change reinforcers periodically to keep the student's interest (avoid satiation).
3. *Successive Approximation.* Analyze the desired behavior to determine if it can be approached by successful completion of small steps leading up to it. For example, Billy might not read an entire chapter. Initially, you may have to reward each step in the following sequence: getting the book, opening the book, turning to the correct page, looking at the page, reading the first sentence, then the first paragraph, and so on.
4. *Contracting.* Once appropriate behavior is being observed, even at a low rate, contract with the student to increase compliance with teacher requests. The wording might be something like: "Billy will begin working on the task requested within 3 minutes after the teacher asks and continue working for 5 minutes without stopping." If this contract is effective, extend it to other requests, possibly in different subject areas. For example, the contract might read, "Within 3 minutes of being asked, Billy will begin working as requested in mathematics, history, and social studies and continue working for 5 minutes." Gradually increase requirements while continuing to reward progress. Consider letting the student select from an array of reinforcers to maintain interest in the tasks. Be sure to simultaneously give low-key praise or some nonverbal form of approval if tangible rewards are given. Pairing of social and tangible rewards allows the tangible rewards to gradually be faded and the social rewards to become effective by themselves.

- *Additional Suggestions.* Reinforce behaviors incompatible with noncompliance using the information presented in Chapter 4 on DRI. When the student responds appropriately to your request, reinforce compliance in some appropriate way. Review the procedures given in Chapter 4 for identifying reinforcers. If noncompliance has been longstanding, teacher attention or praise may not serve as rewards. Tangible reinforcers, such as points or tokens to be exchanged for backup reinforcers, may be more effective.

5. OUT-OF-SEAT

DETECTION Watch for these behaviors.

- Student walks about the room
- Student stands at some place other than her assigned desk
- Student kneels in the seat of her chair
- Student stands beside her chair
- Student sits in someone else's chair

Description. It is necessary to have a clear understanding of what being in one's seat actually means. In most situations, it means that the student's bottom is in contact with the sitting surface of the assigned chair. Anything else is out-of-seat, including kneeling in the seat of the chair or sitting in someone else's chair. For those students who are overactive (see Problem 27—Overactivity), consider a less confining definition of in-seat. For instance, you might consider allowing such a student to kneel in the seat of her desk so long as she is not bothering a neighbor. For a student with severe overactivity, you might initially allow her a defined area within which she can move about so long as she is not bothering her neighbors. The area can be gradually reduced in size as the student gains control over overactivity.

Implications. Being out-of-seat can interfere with the ongoing learning of the student and distract others from their assigned tasks. It should be pointed out that teachers have different views regarding the seriousness of out-of-seat behavior. In some classrooms, freedom of movement without teacher permission is encouraged. It is only when being out-of-seat fosters the noncompletion of required academic tasks that such behavior should be of concern to teachers. An instructional goal is to teach students to remain seated whenever seatwork is assigned or expected. Students are to learn that they may leave their seats only under certain circumstances, such as when permission is given or breaks are scheduled.

Controlling Factors. Students generally leave their seats for a variety of reasons: other things are more rewarding than their assigned task, they have not learned the appropriate time to leave their seats, they have been sitting too long, or they find that roaming around the room brings attention from the teacher and others. For some students, negative attention from the teacher (such as reprimands) can serve to reinforce out-of-seat behavior. In those instances, the teacher is caught in a criticism trap: The more the teacher says "Sit down!" the more the student stands up. The trap occurs because the teacher is reinforced by the student sitting down when she tells her to do so (albeit for a short period of time), and the student's out-of-seat behavior is reinforced by the teacher's criticism (attention).

CORRECTION Try one or more of these procedures.

1. *Determine Where, When, and How Much.* When working with students who are frequently out-of-seat, first determine where out-of-seat occurs. Does the student leave her seat in other classrooms or just in yours? Notice when it occurs. Is it during certain academic subjects, during a particular time of day, or when certain students are near her? Estimate how often it occurs. If the student characteristically leaves her seat only for short periods of time (a minute or 2), count the number of occurrences for 2–3 days. Otherwise, consider using duration or momentary time sampling recording.
2. *Clarify Rules (Instruction).* Students must know what you expect during instruction and during independent seatwork. Consider demonstrating in-seat and out-of-seat behavior. It is reasonable to expect students to remain in their seats during instruction, unless they first get permission to leave their seats for a good reason. Good reasons might include turning in completed work, seeking your help, talking with others about the assignment, getting work-related materials, sharpening pencils, moving on to another activity when the current assignment is completed, and so on. Make sure students know what good reasons are in your classroom.
3. *Schedule Breaks.* Depending upon the age of your students, schedule 2–5-minute breaks every 15–50 minutes. Let students stretch, play, talk, and so on at break time. Praise students for getting back to work immediately after their break. Intermittently provide "bonus breaks" or breaks of longer duration for compliance. For those students who are described as overactive, it is especially important to allow frequent acceptable movement within the classroom. Also, you might watch these students carefully and call on them when you need some activity performed, such as erasing or writing something on the chalkboard, writing on the classroom calendar, emptying the wastebasket, distributing materials, or running errands. (See Problem 27 in Chapter 11 concerning students who are overactive).
4. *Situational Changes.* Require the out-of-seat student to sit near you or where she will not distract others. Consider letting her earn back her original seat after demonstrating acceptable in-seat behavior.
5. *Timer Game (DRA).* Use this game for the entire class or for an individual. Set a timer to ring at various unannounced time intervals, ranging from 1–20 minutes. When it sounds—for example, after 3 minutes (start with short intervals initially)—the entire class earns a point if everyone is in his or her assigned seat. If anyone is out-of-seat when the timer sounds, no point is earned. Sometimes it may be appropriate to withhold a point even if a student is out-of-seat for a valid reason. It is important to avoid attending to the out-of-seat student in any way. When 5–15 points are earned, the class selects a special privilege from a list. Gradually require more points before the class can make a selection.

6. *Self-Monitoring (DRA).* Determine a specified period of time the student can manage to remain in her seat. Then place a chart on the student's desk. The chart might consist of a vertical series of empty squares. Each time the student remains in-seat continuously for, say, 10 minutes, the student colors in or checks a square, starting at the bottom. When the top square is reached, the student is allowed a special privilege immediately or later in the day.
7. *Let Other Students Help (DRA).* Devise a plan wherein the student is rewarded for staying in her seat and working properly for a reasonable period of time. Tell the student that her classmates will also earn a reward. Explain the plan to the students involved. Allow them to remind the student to stay in her seat so that all can earn the reward. It can be useful to use a timer for this procedure. Let the students involved in the plan help decide what the reward will be. But be cautious if you try this procedure. Classmates may complain too vigorously should the student fail to remain seated.
8. *Reward Lower Rates of Out-of-Seat (DRL).* If a student is out-of-seat, say, 10 times per day, let her select from a list of rewards whenever she leaves her seat 8 times or less, then 6 times or less, and so on. Gradually decrease the acceptable number of times.
9. *Paying Fines (Type 2 punishment).* Assign the student 10–20 points or tokens per day. (You might want to review the token system strategy presented in Chapter 4 before using points or tokens as a reinforcer). The student then loses a point each time she leaves her seat without permission. The remaining points can be exchanged at the end of the morning or day for special privileges. Consider asking the student's parents to implement a similar plan at home. Each time the parents receive word from you about an unacceptable level of out-of-seat behavior, the student loses some privilege at home, such as time at play or watching television.
10. *Group Procedure.* Inform students that they will have a 10–20-minute special activity at the end of the day if they leave their seats only with permission. Post a chart for all to see, displaying 2-minute intervals ranging from, say, 0–20 minutes. Tell students that each time someone leaves the assigned seat without permission, 2 minutes will be deducted from the special activity (Type 2 punishment). Whenever someone is out-of-seat, register the loss of 2 minutes on the chart.
11. *Owing Time (Type 2 punishment).* Inform the student that she will owe the time she spends out-of-seat (share your calculations with her). The most effective consequence is to have time paid back after school. If this is not possible, have the student pay back the time during free time, recess, and so on. As a variation, consider combining this procedure with Procedure 6 by giving the student the opportunity to earn points for remaining in her seat and informing her that she will also owe time spent away from her seat.

12. *Earning One's Chair.* Inform the student that she no longer has an assigned seat because she has abused the privilege. Share with her your records of her being out-of-seat. Devise a plan that will allow the student to earn back her chair in exchange for completing assignments. During this time, she must stand or sit on the floor (since she does not have an assigned seat) and comply with classroom rules. It may be wise to secure appropriate consent before implementing this procedure.

- *Additional Suggestions.* As the student learns to remain in-seat, allow her to help you monitor other students who need a plan for remaining in-seat. The student might also prepare a chart of her observations. Playing this role may help her monitor her own out-of-seat behavior. Let the student be a buddy to the other student and allow her to encourage the other student to remain seated.

6. TALKING WITHOUT PERMISSION

DETECTION Watch for these behaviors.

- Student talks out without raising his hand
- Student talks when he should be working
- Student responds before others finish talking
- Student whispers at inappropriate times

Description. The student who talks out without permission makes comments without raising his hand or without approval from the teacher. Problem behavior occurs only when permission to speak is required, not when free give and take is allowed during discussion.

Implications. Students who talk out may monopolize discussions at the expense of others who wish to speak. They may not listen to what others are saying, as they are more concerned with what they themselves have to say. Thus, they may lose the specific points of a discussion, make inappropriate remarks, or repeat what others have said. Related Problems presented in this book are 1—Impulsiveness, 2—Inattention, 12—Interrupting, and 27— Overactivity.

Controlling Factors. Talking without permission has been reinforced by others who allow the student to continue talking and attend to what is said. The student has learned that it is not necessary to obtain permission to speak.

CORRECTION Try one or more of these procedures.

1. *Private Talk.* In private discussion with the student, point out that his frequent talkouts do not conform to class rules. Ask him to practice raising his hand before speaking. You might also suggest that he apply the "Stop, Look, Listen, Act" technique described for Problem 1.
2. *Instruction.* When the student begins to speak without permission, clearly say, "You do not have permission to speak. I'll call on you after you raise your hand."
3. *Situational Changes.* Change the student's seat if he talks to his neighbors too frequently. Consider separating best friends, if talking between them is a problem. However, let them work together at appropriate times.
4. *Differentially Reinforce Appropriate Behavior (DRA).* When the student raises his hand, acknowledge him by saying something like "I'm calling on you, Billy, because you raised your hand to speak."

5. *Reinforce Low Rates of Talkouts (DRL).* After taking a baseline of talkouts, determine the average per hour or some other unit of time. Set the average as the criterion you will accept for the first day or 2. If talkouts are the same or less than the criterion, provide an appropriate social or activity reward; if talkouts exceed the criterion, the student might forfeit points, owe time, or miss some favored activity (response cost). Gradually lower the criterion on successive days.
6. *Ignoring (Extinction).* Make it clear to all students that during class discussion, it is important to hear what several people have to say. To facilitate discussion, each person must request permission to speak by raising his hand. Also make it clear that if a person talks out or begins to speak without permission, his comments will be ignored. Subsequently, when a student begins to speak without permission, attend to a student whose hand is raised and say, "I'm calling on you because you raised your hand. What do you have to say?" Encourage other students to pay attention only to those who have permission to talk. (See related Problem 12—Interrupting.)
7. *Response Cost (Type 2 punishment).* When talkouts are a serious problem, establish a response cost procedure in which the student forfeits a predetermined reward. As a variation on this procedure, use a response cost procedure with the entire group. For example, provide the class with 20 points that represent 20 minutes to engage in a favorite activity. Then list the numbers 20 through 0 on the chalkboard. When any student talks out without permission, make sure that the entire class is aware that it has lost 1 point and why as you erase the top number from the list.
8. *Time Out.* Nonexclusionary time out may be effective. When a student speaks out without permission, take him immediately to the time-out area, a quiet, nonrewarding area in the classroom.

- *Additional Suggestions.* Have the student keep a list of others who talk out at inappropriate times. Discuss this list with him at the end of each day. Ask the student to assess the effects of these talkouts on the classroom activities during which they occurred. Continue to praise the student when he asks permission to talk or when he waits until others are finished speaking before he begins.

7. UNMOTIVATED TO LEARN

DETECTION Watch for these behaviors.

- Student does not begin assignments
- Student does not complete assignments
- Student does not turn in assignments
- Student's work is often incorrect
- Student makes negative comments about school

Description. Lack of motivation to learn is not an observable behavior; instead, it is a characteristic that is inferred from those student behaviors that can be seen. Motivation is a consequence of reinforcement history. The more a student has been positively rewarded, the more likely those rewarded behaviors will recur. When these behaviors relate to school work, we say that the student is motivated to learn. A lack of motivation can be detected by the student's actions, including his verbalizations, such as those listed above.

Implications. The strongest implications of lack of motivation are deficient academic skills, lethargy toward school work, and little interest or curiosity in new things. The unmotivated student may not see the relationships between the curriculum and making one's way in the real world. While such understanding is easier for students nearing graduation, it often provides a challenge when dealing with younger students.

Controlling Factors. Lack of motivation is typically the consequence of the student's past experiences with school work. Usually, those experiences have been filled with failure, for a variety of reasons. The teacher's task in changing the student's behavior is to establish a plan in which school work is correctly accomplished and then appropriately rewarded. In addition, the teacher should determine if any hidden influences are fostering (rewarding) the lack of motivation. (See the discussion of hidden influences in Chapter 1.) For some students, rewards for lack of learning come from their family, culture, and peers in the form of social rewards. These students behave so as to avoid positive social punishment (Type 1) from significant others, such as being called "teacher's pet," "brown-noser," and similar names. In fact, typical rewards, especially verbal praise by the teacher, are viewed more as embarrassing punishment than reward. For such a student, the teacher must determine what types of reward might be effective. It is generally wise to ask the student to list events that might serve as rewards. These rewards are typically tangibles and privileges rather than social praise by teachers. The teacher must be cautioned against thinking that simply because an event is considered a reward by the teacher that it functions as a reward for the student. The teacher might determine if there are students, other than the target student, who are affected by a similar set of rewards. Given that there are, the teacher might use special rewards (e.g., 5 minutes of extra time in gym class) as a reward for the other students also.

CORRECTION Try one or more of these procedures.

1. *Private Talk.* Talk with the student privately in an attempt to determine his feelings and attitudes about his performance in school. It is important not to preach or moralize. Try to identify what the student views as rewards within the school setting. Consider asking his parents about rewards that might be made available at home.
2. *Match Academic Tasks and the Student's Skills.* Consider adjusting the curriculum to the student's skills while keeping a procedure for earning high grades. Some students are unmotivated or turned off because the demands of the academic tasks are inappropriate for their current level of skills. For some students, the academic tasks may be too difficult; for gifted students, the tasks may be too easy and often viewed as boring. For those students who find tasks too difficult, you must make sure that they have acquired all the prerequisite skills necessary for successful completion of assigned school work. This may require a task analysis in which all skills prerequisite to the task are listed. Subsequently, you must determine which skills can be performed and which cannot. Then the deficient skills must be taught before a fair assignment can be made. Also, consider making tasks more meaningful by having them apply to out-of-school interests.
3. *Point System.* Devise a point system as part of your nine-step plan for increasing motivation. Earned points are to be exchanged for the rewards you have identified in your private talk with the student. For these students, play money or tokens might be quite appropriate. (See the discussion of Token Reinforcement in Chapter 4.)
4. *Successive Approximations.* At the beginning of your plan, consider rewarding a rather low percent of correct responses, say, on a worksheet. Initially, an attainable level of correct responses could receive a certain number of

points. Gradually increase the required number or percentage to earn the points and so on up to a standard that is appropriate for the student. Initially, consider making the backup rewards available at the end of the first day. Then make them available after 2 days, then 3 days, and so on until most or all the backup rewards are claimed at the end of each week.

5. *Reward On-Task Behaviors (DRA).* On-task behaviors are defined as those behaviors that relate directly to an assigned or required academic task such as reading a book, writing an essay, conducting an experiment, completing a worksheet, and so on. In this procedure, on-task behaviors are to be increased by offering rewards for time spent directly on-task. (Devise a clear definition of on-task.) The use of an intermittent schedule of rewards is particularly effective here. A timer set at various intervals is easy to use. If the student is on-task when the timer sounds, a certain number of points is earned.
6. *Emphasize Practical Learning.* Devise a rewarding activity that requires the use of newly learned information. For example, if the student learns to correctly solve math problems involving dollars and cents, he can accompany you to purchase Cokes for himself and a friend at a fast-food restaurant. Give the student the money to pay for the Cokes and let him determine if the change is correct. As a variation, let the student determine the area of the gym floor in square feet after he demonstrates in class the correct mathematical formula for determining the area of a rectangle.
7. *Introduce Novelty.* Play a surprise game. Ask for volunteers without telling the students what the task is. Then require that the persons chosen will first have to correctly accomplish some academic task. When the task is successfully completed, let the volunteers do the valued activity. Such activities might be those that allow the students to do something out of the classroom, help another teacher, go with the teacher to another building, and so on.
8. *Social Motivation.* As a variation of Procedure 7, let a small group of students (friends of the student or students who sit nearby) receive a reward contingent upon the on-task behavior of the target student. Activity rewards are frequently successful with small groups. Depending on the age of the students, rewards might be those that foster social interaction, such as listening to tapes or having a "bull session."
9. *Contracts.* Identify several reinforcing activities the student values. Let the student select one of these rewards contingent on fulfilling the terms of a written contract. Choose the terms of the contract so that success is quite likely. Break the learning task into subparts and enter the subparts on the con-

tract. For example, you might have the student correctly spell 3 new words a day for 5 days.

10. *Involve Parents.* As a variation on Procedure 6, ask the parents to help implement a plan in which rewards at home are contingent on the accomplishment of an appropriate learning task at school. A note home each day to the parents tells them if they can permit access to the various rewards.

- *Additional Suggestions.* Ask the student to list out-of-school activities that he would like to do to earn money, possibly during the summer months. For the activities chosen, help the student list the necessary academic skills to do the jobs well. List the requirements in order from least to most difficult. Then set up a special program for the student to achieve the necessary skills. Reinforce the student for each step he accomplishes toward his goal. Offer assistance in helping him find the job he wants.

8. UNPREPARED FOR CLASS

DETECTION Watch for these behaviors.

- Student comes to class with no materials
- Student asks to borrow pencils, paper, or other necessities
- Student is slow to begin work
- Student offers excuses for being unprepared

Description. Students who are unprepared for class do not have the necessary materials and equipment with them to complete classroom assignments. They frequently ask others to borrow a pencil, an eraser, some paper, and any other materials they do not have. Sometimes excuses are given, such as "I forgot," "I lost it," or "The dog chewed it up." Some students, of course, are unprepared for class when they have not completed the assigned homework or other required tasks. In this case, see Problem 10—Unsatisfactory Homework.

Implications. Students who come to class unprepared sometimes experience long delays in getting down to work. These students can disrupt activities requiring all students to participate. Unprepared students may annoy classmates and the teacher by their frequent requests for materials.

Controlling Factors. When the student asks to borrow materials, someone has complied and reinforced the behavior, at least occasionally. It may be the teacher as well as other students who loan or give the student the materials. Some unprepared students may avoid working on their tasks to avoid the consequences, including low grades, a sense of failure, and so on. These students may not be doing well academically in several content areas and may be unmotivated to learn as well. (See related Problems 3—Noncompletion of Tasks and 7—Unmotivated to Learn.)

CORRECTION Try one or more of these procedures.

1. *Private Talk.* In private discussion with the student, determine if there is some hidden hardship factor preventing her from having the necessary materials, such as reduced family finances, a parent losing a job, and so on. If there is a financial reason for being unprepared, consult with the school social worker or school principal to arrange for financial support. Financial support should include money for necessary school supplies. If there is no indication of financial hardship, tell the student that you expect her to be prepared for class every day, just as other students must be prepared. Devise a plan in which she receives some small reward for each day that she is prepared. Gradually increase the number of days between rewards.
2. *Provide Prompts.* Send a note home with the student each day that reminds her to bring the necessary materials to class the next day. The note may be in the form of some humorous sign or a page with a "smiley face". If she fails to bring in the materials after 2–3 days of using this prompt, ask her to have her parents sign the note and return it the next day. As a variation, make 3 copies of materials to bring from home. Post one in the classroom, give one to the student, and mark one for her parents. Have the student and a parent check off materials on the list before leaving home. At school, provide appropriate reinforcement for each item checked off the posted list.
3. *Contracting.* Write a contract with the student that specifies a reward for being prepared for class. For example, the contract might state a number of points to be earned each day the student is prepared. When enough points are earned, they can be exchanged for backup reinforcers.
4. *Owing Time (Response cost).* This procedure is a form of punishment. Explain to the student that for each day she comes to class unprepared, she must owe a certain amount of time. Determine if the time can be paid back after school or during recess. It may also be paid back by not attending some favorite social activity.
5. *Overcorrection.* Obtain approval from the parents and principal to use this procedure before initiating it. When the student comes to school without materials, send the student to the office to borrow half the material. When she returns to the classroom, send her back to the office again to obtain the remainder of the material. This procedure may be effective if the principal and office secretary are reserved in their interaction with the student and if the student misses some favorite school activity while she is in the office. Caution: if the student finds that being out of the classroom is more rewarding than being in class, select another procedure to use.

- *Additional Suggestions.* Establish a class rule that no one is to loan his or her materials. If the target student comes to class unprepared, have the necessary materials available. Tell the student that she may purchase them at cost. If the student has no money or is suffering a financial hardship, consider owing time as the response cost procedure for borrowing materials.

9. UNRULY CLASS

DETECTION Watch for these behaviors

- Noise level in the classroom is unacceptable
- Students are simultaneously talking out, laughing, throwing objects, inattentive, and ignoring directions

Detection. An unruly class is one that is out of control. There are periodic or continuous behaviors, such as those listed above, that disrupt ongoing classwork. Students do not pay attention to the teacher, sometimes acting as if the teacher were not present.

Implications. In an unruly class, there is little, if any, learning or instruction taking place. Not only are most students not learning, but those who are motivated to learn find it almost impossible to do so. In effect, everyone is cheated because teaching and learning are diminished. The teacher who daily faces an unruly class finds the job frustrating and may give up or suffer a loss of self-esteem. In severe cases where discipline is out of control, the teacher may resort to punishment provided by herself, the school principal, or others. The effect of frequent punishment in the classroom is the avoidance of school work, reduced motivation, failure, and anxious students. Many students who find school a punishing place drop out.

Controlling Factors. Behaviors that lead to an unruly and out-of-control classroom are reinforced by peers and by the manner in which the teacher responds to the disruptions: It is fun to be rambunctious and rowdy because these behaviors pay off. For many students, attention from the teacher is a powerful reward, regardless of whether the attention is positive or negative. Students misbehave, the teacher responds (provides attention), and the misbehavior recurs. Unruly classes are usually those in which the students do not know the rules of conduct or the rules are not enforced consistently. Inappropriate curriculum requirements and weak teaching procedures may also be key factors in many disruptive classrooms.

One good indicator of an unruly class is the high level of noise. What might be interpreted as enthusiasm by onlookers may, in fact, be learned behavior taught by the teacher. For example, students may initially learn to raise their hands to gain teacher attention. When the teacher fails to acknowledge raised hands, some students might say, "Teacher, teacher. I know, I know the answer." If these comments are also ignored, the students may begin to talk louder and eventually to shout. They have learned to gain attention by shouting. Needless to say, the noise level in such a classroom is quite high. Some teachers contribute to the noisy situation in still another way. Given an unruly class, they try yelling to gain the students' attention (modeling). If yelling works for the teacher, it might also work for the students (imitation).

CORRECTION Try one or more of these procedures.

1. *Quality Instruction.* A large dose of curriculum restructuring along with quality instruction will subdue classroom disruptions in many cases. If this is a problem in your situation, note the characteristics of effective instruction outlined in Chapter 4.
2. *Establish Rules.* Tell students the rules of conduct in the classroom and the consequences of not following them. If possible, let students help establish them. Specify the rules in a positive way, such as "Talking with permission" rather than "No talking." Don't forget to enforce the rules in a consistent manner.
3. *Provide Prompts.* When the class begins to become unruly, provide a prompt for all to see. One technique is to turn off the lights until behavior is under control. The use of prompts is a preventative measure that serves as a warning before behaviors get out of hand.
4. *Good Behavior Game.* Implement the Good Behavior Game discussed in Chapter 4; read how Mr. Taylor handled disruptions in his classroom.
5. *Reinforce Good Classroom Behavior (DRA).* Provide intermittent rewards for the entire class when behavior is exceptionally good. For example, students could earn additional free time, a special movie, or engage in some other favorite activities. As a variation, give special coupons to the students who are working appropriately. Let these students exchange their coupons for a variety of backup reinforcers or privileges.
6. *Reward Appropriate Attending.* Talk softly so that only the students who are paying attention can hear. Give those who hear you a special privilege, such as "If you are paying attention and can hear me, you may go to lunch 2 minutes early. Raise your hand now if you heard what I have just said." Vary your instructions each time you use this technique.
7. *Owing Time (Response cost).* Establish a response cost procedure in which the entire class loses privileges or some valued activity. For instance, look at your watch or a clock on the wall and determine the duration of the inappropriate behavior. Subtract the time owed from recess, free time, and so on. Eventually, clock watching could serve as a prompt as you say, "That's 2 minutes you owe." Consider having the class help determine the number of points to forfeit or the activities to miss.

- *Additional Suggestion.* Ask students to monitor their classmates' behavior and report on the progress made as a result of honoring classroom rules.

10. UNSATISFACTORY HOMEWORK

DETECTION Watch for these behaviors.

- Student does not turn in homework
- Student turns in careless or incomplete work
- Student does not understand assignments
- Student pays little or no attention to assignments
- Student offers excuses for no homework

Description. Homework refers to assigned tasks that students are to complete after school hours. The tasks are an extension of classroom learning and can be distinguished from extracurricular and voluntary intellectual or academic activities.

Implications. There is considerable disagreement about the role that homework plays in academic and social development. Although research is scant and inconclusive concerning the link between homework and achievement, most administrators, teachers, and parents probably believe that homework is a necessary part of schooling. A logical position is that homework can have positive effects on learners when it is assigned and evaluated properly.

Controlling Factors. Some students simply lack the prerequisite knowledge and skills to complete homework assignments on their own. Others see little relationship between the homework assignment and learning in the classroom. These students, along with those who have already mastered the content of the assignment, are prone to see homework as "busywork" or "a waste of time." Too much homework discourages some students, while others are kept from completing their assignments by such after-school activities as TV watching. Undoubtedly, some students neglect their homework because their teachers assign but do not grade and return it and, unfortunately, because homework has been used by teachers as punishment in the past.

CORRECTION Try one or more of these strategies.

1. *Schoolwide Homework Policy.* The principal, teachers, and parents should formulate a schoolwide homework policy. Provisions to prevent too much homework in a single subject or in several subjects on a single night should be included. Stress the need to evaluate and return all assignments. Arrange teaching schedules to permit compliance with the homework policy.
2. *Letter to Parents.* Send a letter to parents early in the school year, outlining the homework policy. Specify the approximate frequency of homework, how homework will be evaluated, and what is needed in the home (e.g., a quiet study area, a dictionary, and so on). *It may be necessary to ask some parents to control access to play, TV, and other distractors until homework is completed (the Premack Principle).*
3. *Avoid Busywork Assignments.* Do not assign homework as busywork or added work for gifted students. Enrichment is not synonymous with assigning gifted students a greater quantity of work. *Never assign homework as punishment.*
4. *Individualizing Homework.* Consider individualizing assignments. Requiring the same homework assignments from all students is often counterproductive to both advanced and less advanced students. For example, in mathematics calculation, some students might be assigned the task of working on the 12s table in multiplication while others might work on the 2s table.
5. *Prerequisites to Homework.* Provide remedial help for students who need it. All prerequisite skills necessary for successful homework completion should be attained prior to making the skills part of a homework assignment. Arrange for tutoring, if appropriate.
6. *Scheduling Homework.* Avoid last-minute assignments. Outline daily assignments a week or more in advance when possible. Some students prefer working on assignments ahead of schedule. Provide written descriptions of long-term projects well before their due dates.
7. *Making Assignments Clear.* Many students complain that they did not understand what the teacher wanted them to do. While some complaints may be unjusiified, some may be valid. Having a place on the chalkboard only for homework assignments and letting students copy them will usually deter such complaints. When appropriate, include 1 or 2 completed sample tasks.
8. *Purposeful Homework.* Make the purpose of homework and its link with classroom learning clear to all students. When students see the value of homework assignments, they are more motivated to complete them.
9. *Grading Homework.* Tell students how homework will be evaluated and used in determining grades. (Not all homework need be used for grading purposes.) Evaluate and return all homework assignments. It is better to make fewer homework assignments and evaluate them all than to have students turn in assignments and not receive feedback. When grading homework, focus on correct rather than incorrect answers and assign grades as number or percent correct rather than incorrect. Ask your students to correct their errors on homework assignments. The correction of errors could be a separate homework assignment.

10. *Writing Comments on Homework.* Written comments on students' papers can be very motivating. The wise teacher will use written comments with students who do an exceptional job on a difficult task. Comments may also be effective when they are positively stated for those students who are having difficulty with an assignment, even when the resulting grade is relatively low. Such written comments as "You are making good progress" or "This paper is distinctly better than your last" are often unequalled in their motivating force. It is not necessary to make comments on the papers of all students for every assignment. Use an intermittent schedule.
11. *Reassigning Homework.* Reassign critical assignments when they are not turned in or when they are unacceptable. When reassigning homework, consider indicating the number of correct and incorrect responses at the top of the page. But do not indicate which problems are correct or incorrect. Require the students to find and correct all errors. Consider having grades reduced by a certain number of points when homework is late or when it must be reassigned for some other reason.
12. *Charting Homework.* Charting homework completion and grades can provide both teacher and student with a written record of performance. Such a chart can be kept in individual folders for each student or on a master chart kept by the teacher. Information from these charts can be used to report the status of students' homework to parents and others.
13. *Home-Based Contracts.* Because homework is ordinarily completed at home, teachers should seek the assistance of the student's parents when homework problems persist. Home-based contracts for problem behaviors have at least 3 distinct advantages, if they can be arranged. These contracts and their negotiations can

    (a) incorporate a wide range of incentives for completing assignments,
    (b) strengthen communication between school personnel and parents, and
    (c) promote parental involvement in their child's formal education.

    See Chapter 4 for suggestions on writing contracts.
14. *Provide Novelty.* To add spice and vary the homework format, give students the correct answers and ask them to state how they know the answers are correct. Or give your students the answers and ask them to supply the corresponding questions. Consider letting students choose their preferred format from time to time.
15. *Bonus Arrangements.* When students have completed all homework at an acceptable level during a specified period, reward them in some way. As a variation, let outstanding students select 1 future assignment that they do not have to do. The level of acceptance should be adjusted to individual requirements for less advanced students. The teacher should determine the assignments from which students select.

16. *The Good Homework Game.* Assign students to teams whose members are approximately equal in terms of academic motivation and skill. Each team member receives a grade for each homework assignment; A grades receive more credit than B grades and so on. The team with the highest number of points selects from an array of attractive backup reinforcers. As a variation, consider letting each team select a variable number of rewards, depending upon the number of points earned. The team with the second highest number of points, for example, will also be given an opportunity to select rewards but not as many rewards as the first team. You may have to invent some ways to keep team members from giving undue help to other team members. One possibility is to require, in addition to total team points, a minimum team average on a homework quiz.

- *Additional Suggestion.* Ask your students to correct their own or another student's homework. Emphasis should be on providing feedback to the student, not merely grading the assignment. You may need to set aside an area of the classroom to do this. You will, of course, have to provide scoring keys for this purpose as well as carefully formulated rules to monitor the process.

11. ARGUING

DETECTION Watch for these behaviors.

- Student frequently disagrees with others
- Student gets into "yelling matches" with others
- Student is oppositional in many situations

Description. Arguing is verbal behavior in which the student disagrees or takes a stand in opposition to the person with whom he is talking. Sometimes arguing triggers yelling, verbal abuse, and even hitting or fighting (see Problem 15—Hitting and Fighting). Some students who argue seem to do so simply for the sake of arguing; others argue to defend their convictions.

Implications. Most students do not like to talk with or be around a classmate who constantly argues or disagrees with them. Consequently, the argumentative student risks social rejection.

Controlling Factors. The argumentative student has learned to disagree with others because it is rewarding to do so. Rewards can take the form of gaining attention, seeing an adversary upset, being "right," or influencing the thoughts and actions of another person. Some students have learned to argue by imitating others, possibly models found within the family or a circle of close associates. These students have not learned to disagree with others in an appropriate and polite way.

CORRECTION Try one or more of these procedures.

1. *Private Talk.* Talk privately with the student about his tendency to argue with others. He may, in fact, be unaware of the problem. Try to determine the basic function of arguing in the student's life. Do arguments generally lead to increased attention? Or are they mainly to force an intellectual position on others? The answers to these kinds of questions will guide you in your efforts to help the student find acceptable ways to disagree.
2. *Instruction.* Teach the student to communicate with others in an assertive but polite manner. You may find it helpful to consult the literature on human relations training. Someone in your school system (e.g., the guidance counselor) can probably help you locate appropriate training materials.
3. *Teach Debating Skills.* Teach the procedures that are used within a formal debate. Choose topics of interest to students at your grade level or topics appropriate to a subject area for your grade. Ask the student to participate in a debate at some time during this unit on debating. Discuss how some of the techniques can be used in conversations when the student wants to express an idea that conflicts with that of another person.
4. *Ignoring (Extinction).* When the student begins arguing during class discussion, attend to another student or continue the discussion with other students. Teach other students to ignore those who argue in an impolite manner. Ignoring is effective in reducing behaviors when the target student is also reinforced for alternative or incompatible behaviors. Therefore, attend to the student when he expresses an opinion different from others in a polite way or when he waits for others to finish before expressing his opinion.
5. *Response Cost.* Have the student forfeit some reward each time he argues too forcefully. As a variation, require the student to owe time from some favored activity for each incident of arguing.

- *Additional Suggestions.* Let the student who argues to gain attention assume various leadership roles in the classroom such as discussion leader, attendence taker, activity organizer, and so on. Attention gained in legitimate ways may help lessen the tendency to be oppositional.

12. INTERRUPTING

DETECTION Watch for these behaviors.

- Student begins talking before others are finished

Description. Interrupting is talking while others are speaking. The student begins talking when it is appropriate to wait for the other person to finish what he or she is saying.

Implications. One who interrupts too often risks alienating others.

Controlling Factors. Students who interrupt have been reinforced by others who relinquish conversation and then respond to the interrupting student.

CORRECTION Try one or more of these procedures.

1. *Private Talk.* Privately point out to the student that he often interrupts others when they are talking. It is possible that the student does not know how often he interrupts.
2. *Self-Monitoring.* Teach the student to use a three-step Stop, Listen, and Think method of self-control. For example, when the student wants to speak, ask him to "Stop" himself and "Listen" to what the other person is saying. Then have the student "Think": Is the other person finished? If not, the student continues to hold back and listen. The student speaks only after the other person has finished making his point. It may be helpful to roleplay this procedure with the student several times. Praise him (in private) when you see evidence that he is using this method.
3. *Use Prompts.* Some students raise their hands wanting to participate in discussions and feel that they will not be recognized. Consequently, they interrupt. Arrange a signal (such as a nod or a raised finger) to show that you recognize students wanting to speak and that you will call on them after you finish speaking. Have the students jot down a word or 2 to remind themselves of what they had to say.
4. *Promote Good Human Relations.* Teach a unit on conversation manners to all students in the classroom. Point out that it is polite to wait until the other person finishes an idea before saying what one has to say. Have the students discuss how they feel when they are interrupted. Roleplay ways to politely disagree with the point another student has made by saying something like "You have pointed out that ... Another viewpoint might be ..." Also, teach the students to restate what another person has said in their own words. This can improve listening skills. Help the students become aware of their feelings during a conversation. They might ask themselves: Am I becoming angry? Am I being unfair? Create examples where such comments would be appropriate and model appropriate relations. This pro-

cedure is often studied in the framework of human relations training. If you are unsure of the appropriate techniques to use, ask your school counselor or another person who has received such training.

5. *Direct Instruction.* If the student interrupts while you are talking, say, "I'm not through talking. Please wait until I have finished" or simply, "I'm talking, John." Continue with what you have to say and then ask "Now, John, what did you want to say?"
6. *Teach Rules of Debate.* Establish an instructional unit on debate techniques. Choose a topic of interest to the class and choose students to take 2 different sides to a topic. Be sure that all students get a chance to participate in a formal debate. Have the class discuss effective strategies used in a debate format. Point out that some of these techniques can be used in personal conversation.
7. *Ignoring (Extinction).* When the student interrupts you, continue talking, ignoring what the student has said. As you continue to talk, ask the student a question. After his response, reward his waiting and not interrupting.
8. *Response Cost.* Have the student forfeit some reward each time he interrupts. As a variation, require the student to owe time from some favored activity for each incident of interrupting.

- *Additional Suggestions.* When you notice that the student is not interrupting and is using good conversation skills, verbally praise him for behaving appropriately. Have the student make a chart showing how many times he interrupted another student or the teacher each day. Divide the chart into morning and afternoon. Have the student continue the chart for several days and discuss it with you. Consider using a DRL procedure at this point (see Chapter 4).

13. SWEARING/NAME CALLING

DETECTION Watch for these behaviors

- Student uses words or phrases that are offensive to others
- Student calls others derogatory names

Description. Swearing and name calling involve the use of abusive words or phrases when referring directly or indirectly to others. Classifying a word as obscene or derogatory depends upon the situation in which it is used. Words acceptable to one teacher may not be acceptable to another. For instance, exclamations like "Good Lord" and "Oh my God!" are simply the vernacular to some people, while others would condemn this language as cussing and using the Lord's name in vain. Classifying words as unacceptable also depends upon one's tone of voice. "You dummy," for example, could be an expression of endearment or a derogatory statement, depending on how it is said.

Implications. Students who resort to swearing and derogating others risk social isolation and rejection. Teachers who permit such behavior in their classes risk loss of students' and parents' respect.

Controlling Factors. Almost everyone swears or uses derogatory expressions from time to time. Such verbal behavior is associated with frustration, anger, excitement, and fear. Swearing and taunting others are a problem when they occur regularly and disturb social relationships. Abusive language may be largely the result of imitation. The student's friends and associates, and sometimes her family, serve as models for swearing in these cases. Sometimes the student may be unaware of the abusive elements in her speech. Abusive language is also functionally related to the attention that follows its use. Responding with shock or surprise can be especially rewarding to the person who swears or calls others names. Abusive language is also used as punishment. If calling someone "stupid" keeps that person from repeating an aversive action (punishment), the name caller is likely to use similar words for control in the future. Name calling is negatively reinforced in such cases.

CORRECTION Try one or more of these procedures.

1. *Private Talk.* Discuss the student's swearing or name calling in private. Do not moralize. Determine whether she is aware of her use of such language. Identify the specific words that are objectionable and suggest substitute words or actions that can be used in their place. For example, the student can say, "Stop it," "That makes me mad," or "Darn" when she is frustrated or angered. Or the student can ignore someone, walk away, or count to 10 rather than swear. If the student is likely to use abusive language when she is anxious or excited, obtain a relaxation audiotape and teach her to relax.

2. *Situational Changes.* If others in the class swear or use abusive language, make such language off limits in your classroom. Consider posting a specific rule. You cannot expect someone to stop using offensive language if others are allowed to do so.
3. *DRO or DRL.* Consider a DRO or DRL procedure, as discussed in Chapter 4. Consider, for example, letting the student earn a point for each prespecified period of time she goes without swearing (DRO). Or consider providing a reward each day the student swears less than a prespecified number of times (DRL). When enough points are accumulated (require a small number at first), the student or the entire class earns a special privilege.
4. *Ignore Abusive Language (Extinction).* Abusive language is likely to decrease in frequency if it is ignored. Ask your students to completely ignore (say nothing, look away) the student who uses abusive language in their presence.
5. *Owing Time (Response Cost).* The student can owe time (2, 5, 10 minutes) each time she swears or derogates others. Time can be deducted from recess or free-time activities or the student can pay back time after school hours. If several members of your class use abusive language, consider using a group response cost procedure or the Good Behavior Game. These strategies are discussed in Chapter 4.
6. *Time Out (TO).* If the above procedures are ineffective, consider using TO. If possible, use nonexclusionary TO. Rehearse the procedure with the student in private before applying it.
7. *Reprimanding.* If the student continues to use obscene or abusive language after the above procedures have been tried, use reprimands when the behavior occurs. Do not get personal. Refer only to the verbal behavior. You might say something like, "Deb, those words are not permitted in this classroom. Don't use them again in here!" or "Clean up your act, Deb!" Try to deliver reprimands quietly and calmly.
8. *Overcorrection.* Require an apology. The student is to repeatedly apologize to the person she verbally abused and to all others who witnessed the abuse.
9. *Recording.* If all else fails, consider audiotaping the student's abusive language and ask her parents to listen. Once applied, simply touching or even looking at the tape recorder might well prompt the student to stop swearing.

- *Additional Suggestions.* Ask the student to construct a list of positive words that can be applied to others. Praise her when she uses these words in conversation with others.

14. DESTRUCTIVENESS

DETECTION Watch for these behaviors.

- Student damages or destroys property
- Student marks on books, desks, walls, and the like
- Student often misplaces items belonging to others

Description. Destructiveness means deliberately damaging or ruining property. It ranges from placing a mark on something to complete destruction. The damaged property usually belongs to others or to the school. Some students willfully destroy or deface their own belongings.

Implications. Punishment for destructive behaviors ranges from mild reprimands to social rejection to incarceration. When destructive behaviors are reactions to perceived oppression or injustice, consequences of the destructive behaviors may be highly rewarding and any punishment that follows may be viewed as the price one pays for doing what one must.

Controlling Factors. Some professionals maintain that destructiveness represents displaced hostility toward the owner of the property or toward what the property represents. Others say that students who feel guilty for some behavior perform destructive acts to get caught and be punished. Some students have simply not learned that it is inappropriate to damage property belonging to someone else. In the classroom, it is most practical to deal with destructive behavior as it occurs.

CORRECTION Try one or more of these procedures.

1. *Establish Rules.* Establish class rules about respect for the property of others and the punishment to follow when the rules are broken. When a student has deliberately damaged property, enforce the stated punishment immediately. If possible, let students help in designing the rules and the punishment.
2. *Private Talk.* In private discussion, determine whether the student is aware that ownership is to be respected. Discuss, at an appropriate level, the social and legal consequences of destructive behavior. Work out a plan for the student to restore the damaged property.
3. *Situational Changes.* If the student has damaged property using some type of instrument, make the instrument unavailable to the student or place the student where he does not have access to it. For example, if the student uses crayons to mark on walls, books, desks, and so on, remove the crayons from the student's desk. Keep them in a safe place and make them available only at specific times for specific purposes. The student might be permitted limited use of the crayons after performing those activities suggested in the Overcorrection procedure discussed below. Gradually allow the crayons to be used more frequently as the student shows that he uses them properly and in a non-destructive manner.
4. *Bibliotherapy.* Consult with your school librarian and obtain 2–3 books at the student's independent reading level about respecting others' property. Have the student read the books and discuss them with you in private.
5. *Response Cost.* Have the student repair, replace, or pay for the damaged property. If these suggestions are not feasible, consider assigning a comparable-worth work requirement. The principal might be able to suggest things to be done around the school or community.
6. *Overcorrection.* When a student persistently damages property, have him apologize and then repair, replace, or pay for the property. Depending on what property was damaged, have the student repair or clean 2–3 similar items. You must supervise the Overcorrection activities to insure that the student repairs or cleans the items correctly. Do not allow parents to unduly intervene in helping the student replace or pay for the damage. For an outline of overcorrection, refer to this topic in Chapter 4.

- *Additional Suggestions.* Give the student something that belongs to you or to the classroom. Point out that it is to be respected and cared for because it belongs to someone else. Choose an item that requires special care or treatment. Explain that if it is destroyed, others in the class, including himself, will not have the opportunity to use it. After an appropriate amount of time, provide access to a reward if the item remains in good condition.

15. HITTING AND FIGHTING

DETECTION Watch for these behaviors.

- Student slaps, punches, pushes, trips, or kicks other students
- Student engages in physical contact causing pain or discomfort to others, herself, or those involved

Description. Hitting refers to physical acts that inflict pain or make someone feel uncomfortable. When hitting involves reciprocal action, it is called fighting.

Implications. Teachers are probably more concerned about hitting and fighting than most other types of behavior because aggressive behaviors may induce counteraggression in others, disrupt the classroom, and entice other students to act aggressively. Some teachers who work with aggressive youngsters assume that aggressive actions can be therapeutic for these children. They reason that aggressive tendencies must be let out in acceptable ways if the youngster is to engage in more appropriate actions. This line of reasoning has been questioned by some professionals who point out that aggressive behavior, even when expressed in socially acceptable ways, may actually be encouraged if it results in some payoff, such as attention from peers or adults. The best course of action is to deal directly with the observable behavior and work to reduce acts of physical aggression.

Controlling Factors. How one views the cause of aggression determines, in part, how one acts to reduce it. Some professionals think that frustration is the major cause of aggression. They treat aggression by trying to remove the source of frustration, such as lack of attention or failure to accomplish certain goals. Others view aggression as improper learning; they attempt to teach students appropriate social skills.

Aggressive acts are expected behaviors in certain cultures, have been learned at home, or rewarded by peers. (See the discussion on "Hidden Influences" in Chapter 1.) Most aggression occurs because it has been negatively reinforced. The student who fights and hits does so because she has learned that aggression turns off a wide variety of aversive stimulation. The process is similar to that which reinforces scolding or nagging. Teachers or parents soon learn that if they scold or nag a child for something they find annoying (aversive), the child will stop. This makes scolding more likely in the future. Similarly, fighting and hitting work to reduce a variety of unpleasant events in a student's life. Allowing a student to be reinforced in this way may produce a strong tendency to fight and hit.

Aggression also has built in positive consequences. For example, pushing another student out of the cafeteria line in order to get one's food more quickly results in positive reinforcement for aggression. Attention for being a class bully is positively reinforcing also. When dealing with aggression, the trick is to keep it from paying off.

CORRECTION The student who is involved in aggressive acts that result in serious harm to others should be referred to an appropriate professional. For mild cases of aggression, try one or more of these procedures. Start with number 1 and continue in sequence. Use a calm and efficient manner.

1. *Private Discussion.* Talk with the student privately. State clearly what hitting or fighting means and why you are concerned. Does hitting mean punching, finger poking, slapping, and shoving only? Or does it also mean kneeing, pinching, and pulling hair? Ask for the student's cooperation in eliminating aggressive acts. Consider teaching the student a self-control procedure similar to those described for Problems 1—Impulsiveness and 12—Interrupting. You will, of course, need to alter the procedures to fit the case of aggression. Be sure to acknowledge even small gains by the student. Meet regularly to discuss progress.
2. *Situational Changes.* Separate the student from those she hits. For example, change the student's seat or an activity assignment. In some instances, merely being apart from another student with whom hitting or fighting occurs can reduce aggression. If students can learn that behaviors other than hitting are important, aggression may diminish in the process.
3. *Athletic Activity (Situational Change).* Consider involving the student in athletic endeavors such as track and field or gymnastics. An athletic coach could be a key figure in redirecting the student's aggression.
4. *Reward the Absence of Hitting (DRO).* Work with the student to determine a specified amount of time (say, 2 hours) she can manage not to touch or hit someone. Give the student a point or token (and praise) for each period of time without hitting. The points or tokens can be exchanged at the end of the morning or day for special privileges. See the discussion of token reinforcement presented in Chapter 4.

5. *Paying Fines (Type 2 punishment).* Each morning, give the student 10 or more tokens placed in a container. Remove a token each time hitting occurs. At the end of the day, have the student exchange the remaining tokens for special privileges. If parents are willing to cooperate, tokens can be exchanged for privileges at home. As a variation, ask the student's parents to remove part of some privilege at home when hitting occurs, such as less time at play or TV.
6. *Owing Time (Type 2 punishment).* Inform the student and her parents that she will owe five minutes each time she hits someone. The most effective consequence is to have time paid back after school. If this is not possible, have the student pay back the time during free time, recess, lunch, or some other time during the school day. As a variation on this procedure, tell the student that points can be earned for the absence of hitting (see Procedure 4 above). But she will also owe time each time she hits.
7. *Time Out (Type 2 punishment).* A time-out area is one in which there is no opportunity for behavior to be reinforced, either by peers, the teacher, or various events in a situation. The location may be a separate room or even an unused corner in the classroom, depending on the age and maturity of the students. There should be no books or other materials in the time-out area that the student may find interesting. In other words, time out must be much less rewarding than the situation from which the student is removed. See the discussion on time-out procedures in Chapter 4. Each time hitting occurs, send the student immediately to a predetermined time-out area for 5 minutes. If this procedure fails to reduce hitting, send the student to the time-out location for 10 minutes. Tell the student that she will also owe 15 minutes for each incident of hitting, either by staying after school or by less time in some favored activity.
8. *Positive Practice (Overcorrection).* Require the student to engage in behaviors that make appropriate use of her hands, such as filing cards or papers, assembling objects, sweeping the floor, and so on. This activity should last for 2–5 minutes when it is first used. Do not try this procedure unless those listed above have been tried or seriously considered.
9. *Contingent Exercise (Type 1 punishment).* Require the student to sit on the floor and stand up 15 times in rapid succession each time she hits another student. This procedure should be done in private and should be considered a last-resort measure. It will be wise to secure appropriate consent before using this procedure.

10. *Physical Restraint (Type 1 punishment).* Prevent the student from moving her limbs or torso for 2 minutes each time she hits. This method should be used only under extreme circumstances to prevent serious self-abuse or physical harm to others. Be alert to the possibility that physical contact by the teacher could function as a reward for hitting.

- *Additional Suggestions.* Determine the particulars of the student's last aggressive act. Take the role of the student, pointing out how she could have responded without hitting. Consider incorporating into the role these possibilities: walking away, ignoring provocation (looking away, talking to another student), counting to 10, or reporting the incident to an adult. Ask the student to practice the alternatives you have demonstrated or those she suggests as you provide appropriate feedback.

16. CHEATING

DETECTION Watch for one or more of these behaviors.

- Student copies from others
- Student uses "crib notes" during tests
- Student takes credit for classroom assignments others have done
- Student deliberately does not play by the rules.

Description. Cheating is acting dishonestly. Students may copy from another student's papers during tests, use unauthorized notes when taking tests, plagiarize, hand in assignments that are not their own, and so forth.

Implications. Cheating, like lying and stealing (see Problems 17–Lying and 18–Stealing), is often difficult to confirm. Although cheating at times is rewarded (e.g., receiving a good grade as a result of copying answers), it may also lead to negative consequences. For example, the chronic cheater will fail to learn the subject matter at hand, may be labeled a cheater, and risks being shunned by others.

Controlling Factors. Cheating is a learned behavior. Students cheat to make an acceptable grade and to win approval from peers. Other students cheat because they have learned that it leads to an acceptable grade for less effort. It is important to note that when goals set by oneself or others (teachers and parents) are too high, cheating may seem to be the only way to reach them. Even advanced students sometimes cheat because their goal is to make straight A's or to do a perfect job. These students, as well as less advanced students, may think that they have failed if they do not get high grades. Those who make a practice of cheating may hold an unrealistic view of their potential and experience feelings of dejection or lowered self-esteem.

CORRECTION Try one or more of these procedures.

1. *Establish Classroom Rules on Cheating.* Make it clear to all students that cheating is not permitted. Punishment for cheating can range from receiving no credit on an assignment to loss of privileges and failure.
2. *Situational Changes.* When giving assignments or tests that are to be completed within the classroom, remove as many temptations as possible and ask students to sit away from each other. Move about the classroom and carefully monitor performance. Reduce the amount of monitoring when you can.
3. *Situational Changes.* If the assigned work is too difficult, change the assignment to accommodate the student. You might, for example, provide supplementary study materials, require the student to respond in writing to sets of study questions, program the material, assign a tutor to the student, change your expectations, and so on.
4. *Private Talk.* Talk with the student to determine the cause of cheating. Say nothing about past incidents of cheating and state only what you saw. Remain positive and convey the notion that you think the student is an honest person who made a mistake. Do not let anyone call the student a "cheater" if you can help it.
5. *Increase Reinforcement Opportunities.* If the student is capable but under pressure to perform or feels a lowered sense of worth when she does not excel, take steps to reward her in academic and other areas. Increase your interactions with the student. If cheating persists and you think the student is cheating for reasons other than assignment difficulty or undue pressure, consider the following procedures.
6. *Use Self-Evaluation.* Reward the student for accurately assessing her own work. Let the student score a series of her own papers or assignments under your direction.
7. *Withholding Credit.* Do not give the student credit for assignments or tests on which she cheated.
8. *Reassign Work.* Require the student to redo the assignment on which she cheated.
9. *Response Cost (Type 2 punishment).* In addition to Procedures 7 and 8, remove privileges contingent on cheating incidents. If the student's behavior suggests serious and prolonged problems with self-esteem, consider making a referral to an appropriate professional such as a psychologist or a school counselor.

- *Additional Suggestions.* Ask the librarian to select a book at the student's independent reading level about cheating and the problems associated with cheating. If reading the book during class time would be embarrassing because others would see it, assign the book to be read at home or privately in the school library. Discuss the book with the student privately when she has finished reading it.

17. LYING

DETECTION Watch for these behaviors.

- Student makes statements contrary to the facts
- Student often "stretches" the facts
- Student makes others uncertain about what statements to believe

Description. Lying is making statements known or believed to be untrue for the purpose of misleading someone. Some students exaggerate or "stretch" the facts in order to gain attention.

Implications. Lying can have serious consequences for students, such as the loss of friendship and the undermining of a sense of trust between the student and others. Because lying is both hard to confirm and often reinforced, it may be difficult to stop.

Controlling Factors. When students are punished after telling the truth, they may learn to lie to avoid punishment. Lying in these instances is negatively reinforced (see "Negative Reinforcement" and "Punishment" in Chapter 1). Some lying occurs because it has been followed by increased attention or by feeling important and valued by peers or adults. In these instances, lying is positively reinforced. An occasional lie may be little more than imaginative wish fulfillment. Persistent lying may indicate a serious problem in social or character development.

CORRECTION Try some of these procedures. Regardless of the procedure used, avoid labeling the student a "liar." Do all you can to prevent others from calling him names or referring to him as dishonest.

1. *Analyze the Situation.* Try to determine the cause of the student's lying. If lying is motivated by the avoidance of punishment, part of the problem may be in the structure of the class. This is more likely to be true if several students behave similarly (i.e., lie frequently). In this case, you may need to ease off on the demands you make on students. It may be necessary to reduce the amount of punishment as well as the number of threats made.
2. *Avoid Direct Confrontation.* Avoid a direct confrontation with the student, even if you are fairly certain that he is lying. This suggestion is made because the student is likely to respond defensively, you could be wrong, or the confrontation could make an insecure person feel even more insecure. Any of these possibilities could damage your relationship with the student.
3. *Do Not Punish Telling the Truth.* Make certain that the student is not punished when he tells the truth. This does not mean that the student should be absolved from responsibility. If, for example, a student admits to marking his desktop, praise him for his honesty. Make certain that telling the truth brings a bigger payoff than lying. At the same, time let him know that he is responsible for either restoring the desktop to its former condition or making retribution in some other way. He may have to do this during after-school hours.
4. *Reinforce Alternative Behavior (DRA).* If lying appears to be positively reinforced by peers or others, find ways to reward the student for appropriate action. In other words, you must "catch" the student in good behavior. When you notice that the student is behaving appropriately, make sure you reward him for it. This reward can be a simple verbal statement, such as "I'm pleased to see you working so hard on your workbook." This approach can go a long way in building self-confidence and feelings of success.
5. *Response Cost and DRO Procedures.* If you have proof that the student is lying and have tried the above procedures, consider combining response cost and DRO (differentially reinforcing other behaviors). See a discussion of these procedures in Chapter 4. For example, the student could lose free time each time he lies and earn a special privilege for each period of time (e.g., 1 or more days) he goes without lying.

- *Additional Suggestions.* Ask the librarian to select a book about honesty and the problems associated with dishonesty. Make sure that the book is at the student's independent reading level. If reading the book would be embarrassing to the student because other students would be looking on, assign the reading to take place privately in the school library or at home. Be sure to follow this activity with a discussion about the book.

18. STEALING

DETECTION Watch for these behaviors.

- Student possesses things that cannot be verified as her own
- Student claims that she finds the unverified objects
- Student claims that the unverified objects were given to her
- Student is involved in situations where things are reported missing

Description. Stealing is taking the property of another person without permission.

Implications. Stealing, lying, and wandering (not being where one is supposed to be) often occur together. Like lying and cheating, stealing may be difficult to change because it is hard to confirm that something actually has been stolen. The student might make remarks such as "My friend gave me this watch" or "I found this watch in the hall."

Controlling Factors. Usually, things that are stolen are somehow rewarding for the person who stole them. Stealing may arise more or less impulsively. A student might simply take something with little or no forethought. Some students steal to win approval from others by giving them what was stolen ("Look what I have for you"). Others are prompted to steal by a friend or peers. Stealing could be a call for help in the sense that the student wants to get caught. Such students may be in need of attention from you and others. They want to be viewed as important and to be noticed by peers, as do most students. These students might have low self-esteem or negative feelings about themselves (see Problem 31—Low Self-Esteem). Stealing might also occur out of a sense of necessity. Some students steal because they believe that stealing is the only way they can get what they need, such as lunch money, a pencil, or paper to complete an assignment.

CORRECTION Try one or more of these procedures. Avoid labeling the student a "thief," "crook," "robber," and so on, and do all you can to prevent others from calling her names. Do not lecture or scold.

1. *Private Talk.* Talk with the student privately and seriously about her behavior. State clearly what stealing is and why it is important to respect the property of others. Point out that the student would not like to have her own property stolen. Teach the student the difference between *needing* and *wanting* things. Mention that many people would like to have more than they possess. Mention also that when things are purchased with one's own money, the purchased items are likely to be a source of pride and mean more than items that have been stolen.
2. *Return or Replace Stolen Items.* Have the student return or replace the stolen property and apologize to the offended party. You might consider being present when this is done, if the student needs your support. If stealing occurs often, meet regularly to discuss the progress made by the student.
3. *Situational Changes.* If the temptation is known, remove the student from it, if at all possible. If stealing occurs in a specific location, make the location off limits. Arrange the student's time so that she must be at other locations for required activities. If the stealing occurs after school or during leisure time, offer to help the student obtain part-time employment or suggest that she join some organized, school-sponsored, after-school activity. Ask the sponsors of the activity to invite the student to participate. The student could be invited either by the sponsor or by students who participate in the activity.
4. *Clarify the Definition of Stealing.* If the student continues stealing and denies it, see that she clearly understands how stealing will be determined. Point out that a stolen object is any object in her possession not truly loaned to her or that she cannot verify as her own. Let her know that while she may say that the objects were found or given to her, they will be considered stolen. You may need to identify specific individuals from whom things can be accepted. Everyone else would then be off limits.
5. *Increase Reinforcement.* Try to find ways to reward the student for appropriate performance. Often public praise in front of peers is very meaningful. You might keep a list on the chalkboard of students who have done certain tasks well for the day or week. Plan it so that the student's name is on the list every so often. Encourage participation in activities that bring attention from others. Many times, school-sponsored clubs, either during or after school, offer such opportunities for students.
6. *Financial Assistance.* A different approach is called for when a student steals out of necessity. Your task here is to ask for charitable support for the student (and often for the family as well) from community agencies. In addition, you might assist the student in obtaining part-time employment, depending, of course, on her age and maturity. It is necessary that the student return or replace the stolen property, regardless of suspected reasons for stealing.

7. *Reward the Absence of Stealing (DRO).* Assign points for each day the student goes without stealing. Points can be exchanged at the end of the day or several days for specific privileges. See the discussion in Chapter 4 on token reinforcement to help with using points or tokens. Make it clear to the student that all stolen objects are to be returned or replaced and that an apology is to be made to the rightful owner.
8. *Teach Responsibility of Ownership.* Arrange a program in which you gradually allow the student the responsibility of caring for the property of others. Begin with objects that are of no particular interest to the student and gradually include items that may be valued, such as toys, jewelry, money, and so on. Initially assign the responsibility in situations that can be easily monitored and where stealing is not possible. Praise the student for taking care of the property and returning it to its owner. Ask the owner to reward the student in some manner. An example might be keeping watch on some custodial equipment while the school custodian is in some other part of the building. Or consider letting the student keep something for a period of time. Then praise her for returning it. Allow the student to keep items for longer periods of time and take them home. All items must, of course, be returned. Praise honesty and responsibility and tell the student that you knew she was capable of doing what is right.
9. *Modeling and Imitation.* Use a "buddy system." Assign a trustworthy student to a 2-member team to be responsible for the collection of money. Make sure that you have developed the correct procedures and forms that indicate who has paid, the amount of money paid, and so on. Have the students keep the money in some appropriate container and require completion of the forms. Monitor this activity carefully. Reward the students with a highly valued activity, and praise them for their honesty and responsibility.
10. *Response Cost (Type 2 punishment).* In those cases where stealing is known to be a problem and a plan to eliminate stealing has been discussed with the student, give the student a container with a specified number of tokens in it. Each time something is stolen, a specified number of tokens is removed. For older students, points can be used instead of tokens. Tokens or points can be exchanged for a variety of attractive backup rewards or privileges. In any case, the stolen object must be returned to the rightful owner and an apology should be made.
11. *Restitution Overcorrection.* In recurring cases of stealing, fine the student an amount slightly more than the cost of the object stolen. Ask for parental help so that money might be taken from the student's weekly allowance. For those students who do not receive an allowance, determine from the principal if the student could be employed by the school to work in the kitchen or in janitorial services to earn money for the fine.
12. *Referral.* In some situations, stealing persists even after a variety of well-planned interventions have been used. If you find that such is the case with your student, it may be necessary to refer her to an appropriate professional.

- *Additional Suggestions.* Ask the school librarian for a book at the student's independent reading level that concerns someone of approximately the same age and gender on the topic of stealing or other aspects of character. Such books usually tell a story with which the student might easily identify. You should preview the book to determine that it is relevant to the situation. If reading the book would be embarrassing to the student because other students might look on, let her read the book in the library or at home. Discuss the book with her in private. If it seems like a good idea, ask the student to review the book in front of a supportive audience (perhaps another class). Public statements extolling the virtues of various character traits might influence future behavior in positive ways.

19. ANNOYING OTHERS

DETECTION Watch for these behaviors.

- Student talks to others while they are studying
- Student touches, pokes, or bothers others physically
- Student distracts others by making noises, moving about, and so on

Description. Annoying behaviors are those that interfere with the ongoing activities of other students and the teacher. They are unsolicited behaviors. A variety of behaviors can be considered annoying; what is annoying to one student may not be to another. And, of course, annoying behaviors may even be encouraged by some of the student's peers. Many annoying behaviors involve moving about the room, physical contact, and so on. In some instances, the student is not aware of the extent to which his behavior annoys others (e.g., making noises with his mouth, tapping on a desk, rustling papers). When annoying behavior is brought to your attention, you must be careful to distinguish between tattling and genuine complaint.

Implications. Rejection by peers is the major result of annoying others. Because annoying others is intermittently rewarded by various forms of attention, the student may be quite unaware of the negative aspects of his behavior. In fact, even negative verbal comments might function to maintain the student's distracting mannerisms. And because annoying behaviors sometimes take place when the student should be at work on a task, his academic performance may suffer as well.

Controlling Factors. Behavior that annoys others pays off. Attention is the most basic element of this payoff. Another element involves seeing the result of one's actions. For example, certain actions can serve to distract a peer from completing an assignment. The reward for the student in this instance may be seeing a peer reprimanded or keeping him from completing an assignment.

CORRECTION Try one or more of these procedures.

1. *Private Talk.* Talk with the student about his specific annoying behaviors. Point out that he has probably been annoyed at times by certain behaviors of other students. Have him recall the unpleasant feelings he had at those times. This procedure may be effective with the student who is unaware that his behaviors are annoying others. For example, the student may genuinely like to talk to others, but he fails to perceive that talking at certain times can be annoying. You should help the student differentiate between the times when talking is appropriate and when it is not. Modeling such situations might be an especially effective way to teach this differentiation.
2. *Monitoring Others' Behaviors.* This procedure may be useful when the student is unaware that he is bothering others. Have the student list some of his behaviors or habits that he would consider annoying if someone else did them in his presence. He should also list behaviors that others might consider annoying even if he would not. Ask him to observe these behaviors and study reactions to them. Discuss his findings with him. Determine if he can read the nonverbal behavior of others, such as facial expressions, hand gestures, and body language.
3. *Situational Change.* Establish a class rule about not bothering other students when they are working. Teach the students to first give a mild reprimand, such as "Don't bother me now. I'm busy," and to ignore any subsequent attempts to annoy them. Repeat the class rule and post it in a conspicuous place. Be sure to praise students when they comply with the rule.
4. *Response Cost.* In this plan (see discussion of response cost in Chapter 4), the student must relinquish various rewards (e.g., points, privileges, access time to a favorite activity, and so on) whenever his behavior is judged to be annoying. It is crucial to discuss the reported behaviors privately with the offending student. Be sure to discuss what the explicit behavior was and why it was considered to be annoying.

- *Additional Suggestions.* Ask the student to report each time he refrains from annoying others. Show your appreciation in some way.

20. SCAPEGOAT

DETECTION Watch for these behaviors.

- Student is often teased by others
- Others often play jokes or tricks on the student
- Student appears sad or unhappy because others make fun of her

Description. The scapegoat is the student who receives the brunt of jokes, teasing, gossip, and other verbal or physical abuse from other students. It is necessary to separate good-natured teasing from that which is malicious or hurtful.

Implications. Being a scapegoat can result in an erosion of self-concept, social acceptance, and a sense of trust in others. This erosion can affect motivation for learning and may trigger a general avoidance of social situations. The scapegoat may also learn that others will not interact with her in a straightforward and realistic manner. Withdrawal and social isolation may follow in serious cases. Often the scapegoat is asked to participate in some activity, such as a baseball game, by those who know that the "fall guy" cannot perform very well. When she accepts and participates, others make fun of her. The student may respond by feeling embarrassed and unworthy. She becomes an object for others to laugh at and make fun of. The scapegoat may be quite "popular" because she can be counted on to be the brunt of jokes.

Controlling Factors. The scapegoat and those who abuse her are caught in a trap: The more the scapegoat responds to her tormentors, the more abuse she receives. The abusers are reinforced by the reactions they see. On the other hand, the scapegoat may continue to respond to her tormentors because of the attention they provide. Breaking this vicious cycle is the key to an effective intervention plan. (See Problem 5—Out-of-Seat for another example of a social trap.)

CORRECTION Try one or more of these procedures.

1. *Private Talk.* Talk privately with the student to solicit her feelings and opinions about the abuse she receives from others. Determine how motivated she is to terminate their abuse. Be sure to point out that others may abuse her because of her reactions to them. To ease any sense of embarrassment or guilt, mention that everyone is the object of someone's jokes at sometime or other. Be very supportive and make it clear that the situation can indeed be changed and that she is to assume major responsibility for the change. Set up a plan with the student using one or more of the following procedures.
2. *Situational Changes.* Try to arrange social situations in which the student associates with those who do not abuse her. A change of seat assignment can help. Often, however, abuse occurs outside of the classroom, such as during recess, at lunch, in gym, on the school bus, and so on. You will have to solicit the assistance of other teachers who are responsible for the student in these situations. Ask them for their cooperation in setting up a special program to decrease the abuse of the student.
3. *Teach Conversational Skills.* Being picked on by one's peers may be significantly related to the student's inability to communicate. If you suspect that the student is having difficulties in this area, consider teaching her conversational skills in private sessions. Use instruction, modeling, roleplay, and feedback to show the student how to stand erect, make eye contact, introduce herself, initiate conversation, monitor the tone and pitch of her voice, pose questions, make follow-up comments, compliment others, and gracefully excuse herself from a situation if need be. You must be careful to suggest a conversational style that will appeal to the student's audience (peers). It will be wise, for example, to suggest the use of current words or expressions and to avoid outdated ones.
4. *Teach Ignoring.* Teach the student to ignore the abusive behavior of other students. Totally ignoring someone might be difficult for some students. Nevertheless, students who have a long history of abuse must be taught to walk away from physically and verbally abusive situations.
5. *Teach Coping Behaviors.* Set up a plan to teach the student how to respond when others tease or torment her. A plan is necessary so the student will know how to act. Use modeling and roleplaying as the instructional strategy. Teach the student specific things to say, the tone of voice to use, and the body language to exhibit. It is also necessary to teach the student how to recognize situations in which verbal or physical abuse is occurring. After each roleplaying situation, discuss how the student feels about her responses. Reinforce appropriate responses in each roleplaying situation and be supportive and encouraging throughout. In an abusive situation, the student might be coached to say something like "I don't like it when you make fun of me. Stop and don't do it again!" The student should imme-

diately leave the abusive situation. In a situation in which the student has been chosen to participate so that others can make fun of her, have her practice saying "I think you have asked me to do this so you can have a good laugh. Choose someone else!" The student should immediately leave the situation or begin some other activity, join another group, and so on. Be sure the student practices appropriate eye contact, uses a firm tone of voice, and engages in body language that tells others that she means business. In physically abusive situations, have the student practice saying "I do not want to fight with you" and immediately walk away. Teach the student that such assertiveness might prompt names such as "chicken," "fraidy cat," "baby," or other negative terms. If name calling occurs, teach the student to refrain from responding. Point out that she is not, in fact, what these names imply.

6. *Response Cost.* When you witness 1 or more students being abusive, either verbally or physically, respond immediately. Point out that such behaviors are simply not permitted in your classroom. You might withdraw special privileges, some special treat, extra time in gym or at recess, or access to a movie contingent on each instance of scapegoating. Let the students know that they themselves would not like to be the recipient of abuse. It is of great importance that you also positively reward students when they interact with the scapegoat in a socially acceptable manner. A simple positive comment may be all that is necessary.
7. *Teach Self-Monitoring.* Refer to the procedure for self-instruction in Problem 1—Impulsiveness. The steps presented there can be adjusted to fit self-monitoring by students who are subjected to scapegoating. Instruction should be done privately. It includes modeling and roleplaying strategies. The "Stop, Look, Listen, Act" game (also presented in Problem 1—Impulsiveness) can be used. The game can proceed by telling the student to:

    a. "Stop." Do not act if you think the other students are going to tease you. This step is especially important if certain students have asked you to do something.
    b. "Look and Listen." Think about the situation and the intent of what the other students are requesting. Then decide if you should act or not. (You do not have to do something simply because other students have asked you to do it.) If you decide to act, determine how you should act or what you should say in the situation to avoid being made a scapegoat, and then:
    c. "Act." Do what you think is appropriate, such as doing what was requested, making a comment, or walking away from the situation. Notice the response of the other students to your decision.

8. *Teach Self-Defense Skills.* Have the student study any variety of techniques of self-defense. Classes are usually available from local community clubs. Once the student has acquired some skill in these techniques, suggest that she make a report to the class on the topic. Abusing students might stop teasing the student if they think she is capable of retaliation.

- *Additional Suggestions.* Locate literature and film material that depicts man's inhumanity to man. Use this material to design an assignment for those who abuse others. Hold follow-up discussions, stressing the point that everyone deserves humane treatment. Following the discussion, have the students write a short essay about the topic. As a variation, have the students observe others who engage in abusive behaviors and then write a short essay about their observations. The essay is to be written from the viewpoint of the person who received the abuse.

21. SHYNESS/WITHDRAWAL

DETECTION Watch for these behaviors.

- Student is usually alone
- Student seldom volunteers for activities
- Student has difficulty standing up for his rights and communicating feelings
- Student is rarely chosen by peers
- Student may be oversensitive to criticism and discouraged
- Student may verbalize in low tones
- Student may avoid eye contact

Description. The shy or withdrawn student usually causes the teacher little or no difficulty. Thus, the teacher may not see that the student is in need of special attention, especially since the student's relationships with familiar adults are usually satisfactory. The shy student often has difficulty asserting himself. For example, he may avoid volunteering or raising his hand during discussion, even though he may know an answer, and he may turn in incorrect papers because he did not seek to clarify the directions for an assignment. He is seldom chosen to participate in group games. Some shy students seem to be unhappy. Others appear to enjoy the activities in the classroom while keeping their distance.

Implications. Unlike the introverted student who likes being alone while he engages in constructive activities, the withdrawn student seems lost as he engages in solitary but unproductive activities. The shy student often desires the company of others but has difficulty establishing good relationships. The most important implication of shy or withdrawn behavior is social isolation. Severe cases of withdrawal are associated with serious behavioral disorders, depression, and persistently low self-esteem. With this kind of problem, professional consultation and planning are necessary. In many cases, however, the shy student can learn to enjoy appropriate social relationships through a well-designed plan for behavior change. In addition to the procedures suggested below, see also those suggested for Problems 22—Social Isolation, 29—Daydreaming, and 31—Low Self-Esteem.

Controlling Factors. Some shy students have not learned basic social skills for getting along with others. They may even lack knowledge of their basic rights in social situations. In these instances, your task will be to teach appropriate skills for successful social interaction. Other shy students avoid peers because social relationships elicit anxiety that is reduced by avoiding others. Avoidance behavior is negatively reinforced in such instances. With these students, you will have to arrange, in small steps, situations in which they interact with others in ways that lead to positive social relationships.

CORRECTION Try one or more of these procedures.

1. *General Observation.* Review the discussion of observing behavior in Chapter 2. As you make your observations, pay particular attention to antecedent and consequent events. Attempt to determine whether withdrawal is mainly controlled by the lack of social skills, lack of reinforcement because of infrequent social involvement, or avoidance of social involvement.
2. *Private Talk.* Discuss the student's reluctance to participate in social activities. Do not coax or allow others to coax the student to participate. Coaxing might only serve to reward avoidance behavior or to inform the student that he is strange or different. Should you need assistance in detecting social withdrawal, consult with your school counselor. Screening devices are available that will help you identify shy children. As an alternative, consider using a sociometric measure. For example, ask all students to respond in private to a question such as: "Select 3 students with whom you would like to serve on a committee." The analysis of their responses to such questions will yield information about cliques and friendships among your students.
3. *Promote Feelings of Security.* Help the student feel secure in your classroom. For example, talk with him about topics with which he is familiar. Many children will feel comfortable talking about their pets, hobbies, family, and favorite television shows. When you can, refrain from comparing the shy student's performance with that of other students. Make sure that assigned tasks are appropriate for his level of achievement. Analyze his responses to your assignments and alter the difficulty level, if necessary. Tasks should be those in which the student's responses will be at least 90% correct. Try to write words of encouragement on each assignment. For example, you might write, "Great job, Betty. You are doing well," "You have done some good thinking, Eddie," "See what happens when you put your brain in gear! You did a super job, Tom," or "Chico, keep this up and I'll ask you to teach the class!"
4. *Encourage Positive Self-Esteem.* Provide special opportunities for success. See the intervention strategies discussed in Problem 31—Low Self-Esteem.
5. *Make Situational Changes.* Involve the student in group activities. But because social participation may lead to anxiety, move slowly when attempting to involve the student. You might, for example, begin by establishing a procedure that makes use of "helpers" for a period of time (day, week). Place the helper's name on the chalkboard. Select the shy student after several others have served as the helper. In this way, the first helpers can serve as models for the shy student. Helper activities should be those that can be performed easily and can gradually involve the student with others. Activities might include handing out papers, taking attendence, collecting lunch money, and so on. When the student can comfortably engage in

these tasks, provide additional opportunities to participate. In situations in which the class is divided into sections, use the student's name as you make the assignment. For example, "Betty's row can line up first," "These people meet in Betty's area, you people in Sally's area," and so on. Continue to restructure the classroom so that the student has increasing contact with peers. For example, the student might be seated with a supportive peer, sent on an errand with another student, or asked to work on a task with someone who is not too outgoing. Gradually place him with classmates who are more popular.

Expand on the foregoing procedures. Place the student on a team of 4–5 students that is assigned an academic or social task. If you appoint a team leader, do not appoint the shy student initially. Select team members with care, and focus your attention on the group as a whole ("Sally, Allan, Betty, and Jim are really turning out some good puzzle solutions").

6. *Provide Social Recognition.* Display the student's work (academic, art, music, poetry) when you can.
7. *Social Skills Training.* You may need to teach the student to be more assertive. Contact an appropriate professional (school counselor, psychologist, principal, special education teacher, social worker, mental health specialist) for ideas, if necessary.

   Training in assertiveness implies that the student learns to express his thoughts and feelings honestly and in socially acceptable ways. The person who acts assertively stands up for his rights but not at the expense of other people. Teaching someone to assert himself is likely to lead to a variety of social rewards and to an increase in one's sense of well-being.

   You can help the student make his needs known through roleplaying activities. For example, assume that a student (1) lets classmates interrupt him, (2) allows others to push in front of him, and (3) avoids meeting new people. By taking the role of the student, you can show him how he might handle each of these situations. When his talk is interrupted, for example, you might suggest that he say, "I'm not finished yet!" or "Hey, I was talking first!" Reverse roles after each demonstration. In the case of interruption, the student now plays himself, while you interrupt him.
8. *Discourage Negative Private Dialogues.* Shy students may carry on internal verbal dialogues (private conversations with themselves) that turn out to be self-defeating. Such dialogues can disrupt appropriate social relationships. For example, when approaching a group of classmates, the student might think "They don't like me" or "Someone is going to say something nasty again." If the student lets you in on some of these private thoughts, suggest that he replace his negative dialogues with positive ones. For example, when approaching a group of students, he may profit from thoughts like "Remember to smile; make eye contact; pay attention to names; say something positive."

- *Additional Suggestions.* Suggest that the student read a book about social skills, friendship, courage in the face of adversity, and so on. Make sure that the book is at his independent reading level and that you discuss its contents with him in private. If you think it might be helpful, ask the student to review the book for his classmates.

22. SOCIAL ISOLATION

DETECTION Watch for these behaviors.

- Student is not accepted by peers
- Student is usually by herself
- Student is chosen last for teams
- Student is often out of step with peers in dress, grooming, mannerisms, interests, and so on

Description. Social isolation occurs when peers and others do not choose to have a student in their company. The isolated student is usually the last choice for teams and games. She is usually by herself when others are enjoying peer relationships. The socially isolated student tends to differ from her peers in dress, interests, and so forth.

Implications. Social isolation is associated with a lowered sense of worth. At some point, the student who is isolated begins to question her value as a human being and to evaluate herself in negative terms. Often she does not know why she has no friends. Some students may even begin to behave in an obnoxious manner in an attempt to gain attention and approval, only to find that the degree of rejection increases. The social isolate is typically quite unhappy.

Controlling Factors. Social isolation is a consequence of physical and behavioral attributes that others find unappealing. Sometimes peers find one's physical characteristics unattractive (e.g., hairstyle, dress, facial features); at other times, one's behavioral style leads to rejection (e.g., speech mannerisms, clowning for attention). In some instances, the isolated student finds acceptance in a group of associates that the teacher considers as a bad influence or "the wrong crowd." In the environment of her new friends, she appears to be accepted, possibly because she can be manipulated in some way. Sometimes the student who becomes involved with the wrong crowd has an inaccurate perception of the situation; she may think she is popular in her own right, while the crowd makes fun of her behind her back. The primary focus of the teacher of the isolated child is social skills training.

CORRECTION Try one or more of these procedures.

1. *Private Talk.* Being a social isolate is a very sensitive subject with the student and needs to be approached with care and understanding. Approach the topic indirectly when you can. For instance, you might ask the student how she spends her time after school or who her friends are. Try to suggest some situational changes that might help her gain supportive friends. You may have to find subtle ways to help the student change habits of dress, grooming, and so forth.
2. *Observe Student in Social Interactions.* Carefully observe the student in social situations. Note specific instances of her behavior that result in rejection by her peers. Use this knowledge in a social skills training procedure.
3. *Use Sociometric Techniques.* Ask every student to write on a sheet of paper the 3 people they would include in the activities you write on the chalkboard. Choose activities that are appropriate to your grade level, such as "study with," "go camping with," "have on your baseball team," "ask to the prom," and so on. Gather all names and make a sociogram that reveals the "stars" (student most often chosen) as well as the "isolates" (students never chosen). If you are not familiar with how to make a sociogram, ask a school counselor or consult a book about educational measurement and evaluation.
4. *Encourage Interactions.* Encourage the isolated student to take up activities that her peers find attractive, such as drama, debate, athletics, music, journalism, and so on. You will need to suggest activities the student herself will enjoy.
5. *Plan Teams and Groups.* Set up teams and groups for specific academic and social activities. Include the isolated student with others who are likely to accept her. Be sure to reward her team for their group effort. Recognize individual members of the team in front of the entire class.
6. *Roleplay Social Skills.* Given the information you have gathered, identify the student's behaviors that lead to social rejection. Provide private instruction on learning new social skills. Use roleplaying to illustrate both negative and positive instances of the behaviors. If it seems like a good idea, have class members discuss both types of behaviors and how they react to them. Encourage the isolated student to participate in the roleplaying sessions.

- *Additional Suggestions.* Select a mature and popular student with whom to talk in confidence. Point out that you are concerned about the isolated student having few friends. Ask for reasons why others isolate the student and for suggestions to improve the situation.

23. ATTENTION SEEKING

DETECTION Watch for these behaviors.

- Student acts to gain attention from others
- Student often clowns around
- Student acts and talks silly or attempts to be funny

Description. Attention-seeking behaviors, or showing off, are performed for the purpose of gaining attention from others. The show-off is often the class clown. The student who shows off may act silly, talk in an unusual way, tap his feet, snap or strum his fingers, argue, or generally behave in a bizarre or inappropriate manner. Many students show off at some time. We are concerned here with the student who does this frequently and whose behavior is distracting or annoying (see Problem 19—Annoying Others).

Implications. Students who seek attention may not have many friends or receive much attention for other behaviors. The major factor underlying showing off is this: Others attend to the student when he acts in attention-seeking ways. The implication for the teacher is to devise a behavior plan so that attention is received by the student for appropriate rather than maladaptive behaviors.

Controlling Factors. Showing off is reinforced by the attention that accompanies or follows it. Attention-seeking behaviors are typically reinforced by classmates who think the behavior is cute or by negative attention such as being reprimanded by the teacher. Remember that attention can increase behavior even when it appears to be negative in nature. When others provide attention for clowning around, even intermittently, clowning around is likely to recur.

CORRECTION Try one or more of these procedures.

1. *Private Talk.* Privately discuss the behavior with the student. Let the student know that there are a variety of ways to be recognized other than frequent clowning. Be specific. List each unacceptable behavior (giggling, clowning) and, if possible, specify the number of times they occur each day. Let the student know that occasional clowning is acceptable; frequent clowning is not.
2. *Situational Changes.* If possible, separate the student from those who reward his attention-seeking behavior. Consider combining this strategy with one that rewards those who ignore clowning and showing off.
3. *Reward Alternative Behavior (DRA).* Ask the student to help you take attendence, distribute materials, collect homework, monitor class activities, and so on. These activities may provide needed and appropriate attention from you and the student's peers.
4. *Response Cost or Time Out (Type 2 punishment).* If the first 3 procedures fail to reduce attention-seeking behaviors, consider implementing a response cost or time-out procedure immediately after the student begins to show off. The student could owe 5 minutes of free time each time he shows off (response cost) or be placed in time out at the beginning of each incident. If neither of these procedures works, consider using them together.
5. *Negative Practice (Type 1 punishment).* When the student begins clowning, whisper to him that he will have to stay in at recess or after school for a period of time. When all classmates are gone, require him to practice showing off repeatedly in the empty classroom.

- *Additional Suggestions.* Encourage the student to take up activities that draw appropriate attention from others, such as drama, athletics, music, radio or television announcing, and so on.

24. BABY TALK

DETECTION **Watch for this behavior**

- Student uses language that is immature for his age

Description. Baby talk is language that is grammatically and syntactically similar to that of a much younger student. Note that articulation difficulties, such as substitutions ("wabbit" for "rabbit"), omissions ("ovie tar" for "movie star"), and distortions ("schlip" for "ship") are not considered within this definition. Articulation difficulties are problems apart from baby talk and need to be remediated by a certified speech and language pathologist. Examples of baby talk are "Me can do this," "My mommy loves me," "Betty Sue feels sick" when referring to self, and so on. Again, baby talk is not due to language or articulation disorders or to language delays requiring specialized professional remediation. The student who engages in baby talk is quite capable of correct language usage.

Implications. Even though the student who talks like a baby may think it's cute or coy, baby talk can lead to negative reactions from others. These reactions may go unnoticed by the student who baby talks.

Controlling Factors. Baby talk is used by young students because of the attention it cues in others, especially from family members. This attention usually began when the student was very young and continued as oral expression developed through the preschool years. Baby talk is especially noticed when the student first enters school. In some cases, it continues well into the second and third grades. Most often, the use of baby talk is diminished because of teasing and other environmental influences. Nevertheless, it is a behavior that occurs with enough frequency to be a problem in the social development of some students.

CORRECTION Try one or more of these procedures.

1. *Private Talk.* Privately explain to the student that some of his language usage is unacceptable for his age. Try to determine why he uses baby talk. He may be unaware of his baby talk because it has been acceptable to others in the past. If possible, identify specific expressions that are to be off limits. Be careful not to preach or to embarrass the student.
2. *Ignore Baby Talk.* Refrain from attending to the student in any way each time he uses baby talk in your presence.
3. *Model Correct Language Usage.* When you hear the student use baby talk, audiotape, write down, or remember what was said. After you have 2–3 examples, plan a private discussion with the student. Model correct language usage for him, using the examples. Have the student say the sentences or language patterns in the correct way. Reinforce the student's correct responses. Encourage the student to continue using correct language.
4. *Response Cost.* Tell the student that he will have to forfeit a certain number of points or that he will be denied certain privileges when he uses baby talk. See the discussion of response cost in Chapter 4.
5. *Parent Involvement.* Arrange for a parent conference and discuss with them the student's use of baby talk. Try to determine if they reinforce such language at home. Solicit their participation in a plan to decrease the student's baby talk. Determine what reinforcers they can use at home when the student uses appropriate language and what privileges can be withheld when baby talk is used. Set up a plan for them to follow that both decreases baby talk and increases correct language usage. This plan might incorporate features of Procedures 2, 3, and 4 above.

- *Additional Suggestions.* In the presence of the target student, compliment other students for speaking in a grown-up fashion.

25. TATTLING

DETECTION Watch for these behaviors.

- Student tells secrets or gossips about others
- Student informs you about trivial behaviors of others
- Student makes negative or critical comments about peers

Description. Tattling involves telling others about the whereabouts or actions of another in an effort to provoke a negative evaluation of the other person or to gain approval for oneself.

Implications. Tattling can interfere with the establishment or maintenance of friendship. The tattler may be thought of as untrustworthy. It is important to teach students the difference between tattling and informing adults in appropriate situations: When someone is hurt, when someone is in a dangerous situation, or when property is being damaged. The general task for the teacher will be to see that the student receives the attention of adults and peers for appropriate behaviors, not for tattling.

Controlling Factors. Tattling is largely controlled by the attention one receives for doing it. Some students enjoy the sense of control over other people's lives that might occur as a result of tattling. Tattling might also indicate that the student feels excluded from a group or, on rare occasions, that he secretly desires to participate in the activities that are the subject of the tattling.

CORRECTION Try one or more of these procedures.

1. *Private Talk.* Teach the student the difference between tattling and reporting potentially dangerous situations. Provide plenty of examples of tattling and appropriate informing. Try to provide the student with extra opportunities that lead to success and attention from others.
2. *Situation Change.* Determine whether tattling is related to being excluded from a group. If so, try involving the student in various small-group activities that are of interest. For example, the student might be assigned to a group that has a particular responsibility or project that is appealing to the students. By being a part of a group, the tattler might feel a sense of belonging and importance. Chances are that when the student feels a sense of membership, the tendency to tattle will diminish.
3. *Reinforce Alternative Behavior (DRA).* Praise the student when he makes positive comments about other students. Point out that positive comments help promote good human relations. In addition, arrange for the student to receive your praise and positive attention from peers for a variety of appropriate classroom behaviors.
4. *Reward the Absence of Tattling (DRO).* Set up a plan to periodically reward the student for not tattling. For example, you might plan to use praise if the student has not tattled for some predetemined period of time. If tattling occurs, say, twice daily, praise the student at the end of the morning and the end of the afternoon if he has not tattled. Make a point of complimenting the student when he talks positively about others.
5. *Ignoring.* Tell the student that you will not acknowledge his tattling. Then withhold all attention when tattling occurs. This means not looking in the student's direction and not saying *anything* at all. Be sure to differentially reward the student for other appropriate behaviors. (See the discussion in Chapter 4 on the premier strategy, DRA).
6. *Response Cost.* Remove a small reward each time tattling occurs. For instance, deduct 5 minutes of recess time for each tattling episode. Continue to differentially reinforce the student for appropriate behaviors.

- *Additional Suggestions.* Be alert to the possibility that students who engage in frequent tattling and criticism of others may have a low opinion of themselves. See Problem 31—Low Self-Esteem for suggested procedures.

26. TEMPER TANTRUMS/CRYING

DETECTION **Watch for these behaviors.**

- Student throws self on floor and yells, kicks, and screams
- Student loses control and engages in outbursts of anger
- Student swears, whines, cries, stomps, hits, and throws things
- Student cries and whimpers to get her way

Description. Temper tantrums are often accompanied by physical waving of arms, hitting, yelling, screaming, pounding objects, and crying. Crying involves uttering sounds of pain or distress, shedding tears, and sobbing (catching one's breath). It is important to distinguish between crying in response to painful or punishing events (falling down and hurting oneself) and crying for attention or to get one's way. Crying because of pain or punishment can be interpreted as a call for help. Crying for attention or to get one's way may be interpreted as a possible problem behavior; they are of concern here. Most temper tantrums are exhibited by preschool and early-elementary-school children. Tantrums in older students are indicative of immaturity in most cases, although behaviors similar to temper tantrums may be observed in situations where a student feels intense fear or panic.

Implications. The student who engages in chronic tantrums and crying episodes (two or more per week) is likely to delay classroom teaching and learning activities. Later these students may be embarrassed by their own actions. They need to learn appropriate ways to get attention and cope with frustration and anger.

Controlling Factors. Although in rare cases temper tantrums and crying for attention may be due to physical illness, these behaviors are most often the result of the various forms of attention that follow them (positive reinforcement). Some students have learned that tantrums allow them to get out of doing things (negative reinforcement) or gain them access to tangible and activity rewards (positive reinforcement). It is important to note that a vicious cycle may exist: The student who engages in tantrums is rewarded, while the person giving in to the tantrums is negatively reinforced for doing so (something annoying or disturbing is temporarily eliminated). Tantrums are likely to occur when the student is told she must do something she does not want to do or when she is denied access to something.

CORRECTION Try one or more of these procedures.

1. *Private Talk.* Discuss the student's temper tantrums or crying with her. Let her know that you are concerned about the frequency of her outbursts and that she cannot cry and carry on to get what she wants. Be specific. List the unacceptable behaviors: crying, pounding, yelling, throwing things, and so on. Do not imply that crying itself is wrong or bad. Discuss alternative ways for the student to get what she wants.
2. *Withhold Attention (Extinction).* If possible, withhold all attention. Unless danger is involved, apply this procedure in *every* case.
3. *Differentially Reinforce Other Behavior (DRO).* Reward the student for the absence of tantrums. A child could earn a star, to be exhibited on a chart, each time she goes half a day, say, without a tantrum. When enough stars are accumulated (require a small number at first), she or the entire class earns a special privilege.
4. *Time Out (TO).* Time out means time out from reinforcement (see the discussion of TO in Chapter 4). Place the student in TO in the back of the room at the start of each tantrum (nonexclusionary TO). Remember to totally ignore her behavior while she is in TO. Require the other students to do the same. If necessary, provide special privileges to students for paying no attention (looking away, saying nothing) to the outbursts. Beware that when an outburst is first ignored, things may get worse before they get better. Your task and that of your students is to ignore the behavior, difficult as it may be. If the student is causing physical damage to herself or others, hold her fast in her seat for several minutes, while other students continue to ignore the behavior. Be aware that your attention and physical closeness in this circumstance might serve to reinforce the student's self-injurious or aggressive behavior. Therefore, it may be necessary to implement exclusionary TO in which the student is removed from the classroom to a very boring location. Simply tell the student why TO is being used and take or direct her to the area. Have her clean up any mess made while in TO.
5. *TO and Owing Time (Response cost).* Add a response cost procedure to TO. For example, each time the student misbehaves, place her in TO *and* remove a reward (time from recess, free time, and so on).
6. *Overcorrection.* Overcorrection involves punishment and reeducation (see the discussion in Chapter 4). If none of the above procedures are effective, try requiring repetitive apologies for each outburst, or require the student to repeatedly make a proper response to a demand (positive practice). If the room has been disturbed during the tantrum, have the student restore it to its former condition and tidy up the rest of the room as well (restitution).

- *Additional Suggestions.* When the student responds appropriately to a frustrating situation, praise her for it. Try to reward the student for appropriate behavior as much as you can. Teach her that she can get what she wants by following rules and the suggestions in Procedure 1 above.

27. OVERACTIVITY

DETECTION Watch for these behaviors.

- Student seems to be constantly on the go
- Some part of the student's body is constantly in motion
- Student finds it difficult to sit still for any length of time
- Student requires much space for moving about

Description. Overactivity is fine-motor and gross-motor movement exceeding what is considered normal for the student's age. The definition of overactivity will vary with those who define it. For instance, one teacher may label a student overactive, while another teacher might call the same student "bubbly." There are no written tests to measure overactivity; we must rely on direct observation. Any definition of overactivity should be validated by having several teachers or observers record the student's behavior using the same definition. If consensus is reached, the definition can be used. Since younger students are generally more naturally active than older students, age and maturity level must be considered before labeling any student overactive. When trying to decide if the student is overactive, other factors to consider are (1) the characteristics and difficulty level of required academic tasks and (2) the situational and social circumstances. For instance, if the tasks are too difficult, students will find ways to avoid them, often by being overactive. It is not necessarily appropriate to require students to sit perfectly still, to stand up straight, or to refrain from talking. Given the wide range of acceptable or normal movement for each age level, the teacher should recognize this fact rather than being too quick to label a student overactive. Excessive movement should be reduced when it interferes with accomplishing academic tasks or occurs when quiet behavior is appropriate or required.

Implications. The overactive student often annoys others merely by his presence. He may not know his behavior is annoying (see Problem 19—Annoying Others). The consequence of such behavior is often social rejection and isolation by peers. An overactive student may fail to attend to stimuli or events, be they books, movies, class discussions, or instructions from the teacher. The student thus misses out on assigned tasks, turns in incomplete or incorrect work, and receives low grades. Certainly, these deficits are not characteristics of all overactive students. Some overactive students wander about the classroom, stare out the window, sharpen pencils, or go

Controlling Factors. Some professionals believe that a high degree of overactivity, sometimes called *hyperactivity*, is caused by neurological or physiological factors; other professionals believe that overactivity is a response to environmental stimuli; yet other professionals feel that overactivity might be the result of certain controlling emotional factors. Our position in this book is that most overactivity in classrooms is largely a matter of learning and can be modified by using a systematic behavior change plan. However, it is important to note that a very high rate of overactivity requires appropriate professional assistance. Although medication might be an appropriate part of treatment in severe cases, it should be used with restraint. It is crucial that the behavior of students on medication be monitored by the teacher. Any marked deviation from previous behavior must be reported to the student's parents and his physician.

CORRECTION Try one or more of these procedures.

1. *Label the Problem Correctly.* Make sure that the label *overactive* is correct for the target student. See the above discussion under *Description*. Once you decide that the label is appropriate, consider implementing the following procedures. Report effective procedures to others who have responsibility for the student.
2. *Situational Change.* Arrange a study carrel that blocks out distracting visual stimuli. The carrel can be assigned as the student's "office" to be used for academic tasks. It is a good idea to have several carrels for other students who want a private space for doing their work. Shipping boxes for refrigerators make excellent carrels.
3. *Change Situation.* Place the student away from distractions as much as possible. For instance, place the student's desk so it does not face windows or doors and is away from distracting neighbors.
4. *Program Movement.* Plan situations in which the student is given permission or required to move about. For instance, engage the student in tasks requiring mobility, such as standing up when answering a question, writing on the chalkboard, demonstrating examples or sample activities, washing the chalkboard, passing out papers, taking notes to the principal, taking the wastebasket to the custodian, dusting erasers, and so on. Do not require the student to sit in one place too long. Some overactive students may not be able to remain seated for more than a few minutes. Assign these students a task requiring movement *just before* they have an urge to leave their seats. As a variation, work out a signal, such as a nod, giving the student permission to move about the room for a brief period of time.

5. *Instructional Variety.* Plan short instructional lessons and tasks. Allow a brief transition or relaxation period between them. Make every lesson as different from the preceding one as possible. For example, follow independent work with group work. Then use independent work followed by work in pairs. Variety is the key here.
6. *Accommodate Learning Style.* Determine the factors that facilitate and interfere with comfortable, correct, and efficient learning. Some students like to see characteristics, outlines, shapes, letters, words, and pictures. They often use notes, drawings, and coloring to highlight the "visualness" of the task. Others find these approaches distracting, preferring to listen, discuss, and talk about what is to be learned. Some students prefer independent work while others prefer large- or small-group instruction. Some students like to listen to various types of music while others must have silence while they are learning. Ask the student to describe his preferences when studying and learning. Try to accommodate as many of these preferences as you can. For example, study carrels can eliminate some visual distractions. Allowing the student to use a portable headset with radio or cassette might be of benefit while other students might want to use earplugs to block out auditory distraction.
7. *Reinforce Alternative Behavior (DRA).* Reinforce behaviors that are appropriate when the student is not being overactive. After a short period of time in which the student refrains from overactivity, spend some time with him, possibly reviewing a lesson or simply talking about something he enjoys. For younger students, free time in which lots of movement and yelling is permitted can be given after the student quietly attends to the teacher for some period of time. This procedure works if the student values movement and yelling. It illustrates the Premack Principle, discussed in Chapter 3.
8. *Self-Instruction.* Modify the "Stop, Look, Listen, Act" procedure given in Problem 20—Scapegoat. Be sure to model the procedure for the student and have him practice the steps.
9. *Increase Tolerance (Ignoring).* Try to ignore overactive behavior that is nondisturbing and noninterfering. This strategy is difficult for some teachers. The best way to ignore behavior is to literally turn your back on it; look the other way and say nothing. Be aware that you can reinforce behavior by the expression on your face as well as by what you say. Teach other students to ignore overactivity, and reward them as a group for doing so. For example, if they do not attend to the student when he is particularly overactive, the entire class is to receive extra time at recess. (The overactive student should not receive extra time.) If the overactive student is seated away from others, ignoring is facilitated.
10. *Contracts.* Let the student have input into the terms of a contract you write with him. Consider the student's level of overactivity so that the terms are not too demanding initially.

11. *Timer Game.* Set a timer to ring at various unannounced time intervals, ranging from 1–30 minutes. When it sounds, for example, after 3 minutes, the student earns a prespecified number of points or tokens if he is on-task and not engaged in overactive behavior. Be sure to set the timer at short intervals initially. Gradually require more points to be exchanged for valued backup reinforcers.

- *Additional Suggestions.* Talk with the student and his parents about extracurricular activities that require movement, such as gymnastics, track and field sports, swimming, and so on. These activities may help reduce overactivity in some students.

28. OVERDEPENDENCE

DETECTION Watch for these behaviors.

- Student requests assistance from others repeatedly
- Student frequently asks questions of peers or teacher
- Student solicits opinions from others before making decisions
- Student stays close to the teacher
- Student does not want to share the teacher with others

Detection. Overdependence is excessive reliance on others to provide direction, guidance, or answers to questions. Overdependence is immature behavior. Most students assume more and more responsibility for their own behavior as they get older, rather than depend on others to make their decisions. The overdependent student can be very frustrating to the teacher because it seems that she is constantly interrupting, asking questions, or staying too close. The student acts helpless and may verbalize that she cannot do the assignment.

Implications. Students who are overdependent do not develop independence at a rate that is appropriate for their age. In addition, persistent calls for help may alienate others.

Controlling Factors. Overdependence is a learned behavior because it has been reinforced by those on whom the student is dependent. When dealing with an overdependent student, it is important that the tasks presented are those that the student can perform with a minimal amount of instruction or guidance. Some overdependent students have learned to ask questions because assigned tasks have been too difficult or unclear. Sometimes, prerequisite skills have not been acquired. Overdependence is rewarded because it assures the student that she will not fail; others will do the task for her. Sometimes, too, overdependence is fostered by adults who are unwilling to relinquish control over the life of a child.

CORRECTION Try one or more of these procedures.

1. *Private Talk.* Discuss with the student why her overdependent behavior is so frequent. Determine whether academic tasks are appropriate for her level of achievement. Determine whether she is afraid of failure and what the consequences of failure might mean to her. Possibly, her parents are demanding performance at an inappropriately high level or maybe she has set her own standards unrealistically. Maybe overdependent behavior is the only way she knows to receive attention.
2. *Explanation of Tasks.* After you give instructions to the student or to the class, ask if there are any questions about the assignment, when it is due, and any other particulars. Be sure the assignment is clear to everyone. When the overdependent student asks a question about the assignment, instead of giving the answer, ask her to tell you what she understands the assignment to be. If her understanding is correct, tell her that she is accurate and no further instruction is needed. Make sure that she can perform the tasks after an appropriate degree of instruction.
3. *Differentially Reinforce Alternative Behavior (DRA).* Be certain to reward those behaviors that suggest independence of action. This procedure is especially important when you also ignore dependent behaviors. For example, you might establish a number of points to be assigned for specific tasks that are completed without asking questions or being dependent on others. The points can be exchanged later for backup reinforcers that the student values.
4. *Ignoring.* Ignore the student's requests for help when you are reasonably certain that she is capable of responding on her own. Say something like, "I think you can figure that out yourself." Then say nothing more.
5. *Successive Approximations.* If the student is so overly dependent that she cannot perform a simple task without assistance, break the task down into smaller sequential steps that can be performed independently, and reward each step along the way. Provide a special reward when the task is finally accomplished. Consider telling others of her accomplishment.
6. *Response Cost.* Response cost procedures (see Chapter 4) are effective when a student persists in making unnecessary requests.

- *Additional Suggestions.* Try a DRL procedure. First, clearly define what you mean by overdependence. Second, make certain the student understands the definition. Finally, supply a small reward each time the student falls at or below a prespecified standard (say, no more than 10 dependent incidents per day). The standard can be gradually lowered in steps as the student learns to be more independent.

29. DAYDREAMING

DETECTION Watch for these behaviors.

- Student frequently stares out the window instead of working
- Student gazes into space instead of looking at materials
- Student appears to be thinking about something other than the task

Description. Daydreaming is a private event during which attention is focused on something other than tasks or task-related activities within the environment. The daydreamer is usually not looking at or bodily oriented toward appropriate stimuli. The daydreamer may be described as "dawdling" or not paying attention (see related Problem 2—Inattention).

Implications. According to some, students who frequently daydream desire to live in fantasy rather than face reality. Indeed, daydreaming often occurs in situations that are stressful or unappealing to the student for some reason. Because of his daydreaming, the student often fails to complete work on time, does the wrong assignment, or misses information that is presented during instruction or classroom discussions. Thus, frequent daydreaming can result in lowered academic performance.

Controlling Factors. Because daydreaming is a private event, it is difficult to identify the controlling factors. Usually, one daydreams to avoid unpleasant environmental circumstances (negative reinforcement), to experience exciting and pleasant thoughts and images (positive reinforcement), or to mull over a variety of real and imagined problems. It's often easier to fantasize than face the stressful demands of the classroom. Private thoughts can be quite exciting, pleasing, and reinforcing.

CORRECTION Try one or more of these procedures.

1. *Private Talk.* In private discussion, try to discover why the student engages in frequent daydreaming. Solicit the student's opinion about classroom assignments and their level of difficulty for him. Determine if hidden influences might be affecting his daydreaming. Be on the lookout for family situations that might be distracting the student. Once this information is obtained, establish a plan to diminish daydreaming by using one or more of the following procedures.
2. *Analyze Academic Requirements.* Determine if the school work is at an appropriate level for the student. It may be that the tasks are too easy or much too difficult. Tasks that are too difficult can provoke an escape into daydreaming. Those that are too easy might induce boredom and do the same. Make sure that the tasks provide an appropriate degree of challenge requiring concentration to complete.
3. *Schedule Interesting Tasks.* Determine the student's interests. This can be done through private talk or by using a formal or informal interest inventory. Try to assign these tasks at times when the student is especially prone to daydream.
4. *Use Cues.* When you see the student daydreaming, Use his name in an example or call his name and simply ask a question such as "Are you with us?" It might be unfair to ask him a question about the class discussion if you are reasonably sure that the student has been daydreaming. Your purpose is to get the student to refocus his attention on the task at hand.
5. *Self-Recording.* Teach the student to determine how long he daydreams each day (duration recording). He must learn to record the time at the first signs of daydreaming and at the end of each daydreaming episode. Self-recording can be a big help in changing behavior, especially when it is combined with other intervention procedures.
6. *Consider the Premack Principle.* Design a plan that provides time to daydream as a reward for the completion of required tasks. If daydreaming is preferred over required tasks, such a provision is an application of the Premack Principle described in Chapter 3.

- *Additional Suggestions.* Rather than concentrate on the student's daydreaming, focus your attention on task completion. Increasing task completion may well reduce time spent daydreaming.

30. HYPERSENSITIVITY

DETECTION Watch for these behaviors.

- Student's feelings are easily hurt
- Student is easily embarrassed or upset when teased
- Student is fearful of situations and events
- Student cries or pouts after making mistakes

Description. Hypersensitivity refers to overreacting to events that most people would simply ignore. The hypersensitive student gets her feelings hurt easily or becomes upset over what appear to be minor frustrations. A negative comment, for example, may elicit anxiety and crying. Almost everyone is upset on occasion by events that turn out to be quite minor. But hypersensitive students experience a series of setbacks that make them feel quite uncomfortable.

Implications. Hypersensitivity may be a serious problem for a student who is repeatedly upset over minor frustrations. It would be wise to consult with an appropriate professional in this case. Hypersensitive students may be the target of jokes and teasing. This, of course, can make matters worse.

Controlling Factors. Hypersensitive reactions have probably been learned early in the student's life. The student may have learned to feel a sense of shame, inadequacy, or incompetence in response to early experiences with family members and other important people in her life. The major goal of intervention is to teach the student how to cope with the setbacks and disappointments everyone experiences.

CORRECTION Try one or more of these procedures.

1. *Private Talk.* Approach the discussion carefully. Try to determine how often the student feels badly, what situations or specific students provoke these feelings, and how she feels about her reactions.
2. *Situational Changes.* If the student is very young, place her away from those who tease or provoke her. Assign the student to groups who do not aggravate her.
3. *Clarify Rules.* Make it very clear to all students that you will not tolerate behaviors that tease, provoke, or make fun of other students. Establish procedures for handling such provocation.
4. *Increasing Successful Performances.* Arrange academic and social situations so that the student will be successful. Be certain that the academic tasks required are at a level where success is likely. When a student earns a good grade for these academic tasks, reward her immediately, enthusiastically, and verbally in the presence of others. Discern what particular and unique talents the student might have that would be valued by peers. Allow the student to use these talents in a special class project.
5. *Teach Self-Talk.* Teach a procedure to use in situations where the student feels upset:
   (a) Determine if the situation is tense.
   (b) Evaluate the situation by repeating what is occurring. For example, she might say to herself, "Billy is trying to upset me."
   (c) Use self-instruction. Have the student say to herself something like, "I won't cry or feel embarrassed by Billy's talk."
   (d) Walk away from the situation. Have the student move to a different location or engage in some behavior that requires a different focus of attention.

   To teach the student these techniques, first model self-talk and have the student repeat after you. Then roleplay a potentially tense situation in which you are the teasing student and the target student plays herself. Have the student verbalize the self-talk. Correct and praise her efforts.
6. *Reinforce Approach Behaviors.* Reward closer and closer approaches to the situation or event in which the student feels tense. Because reinforcement can elicit positive feelings as well as strengthen approach behaviors, this is potentially a very effective procedure. The key is to *gradually* approach tense situations while providing reinforcement at each step.

- *Additional Suggestions.* When you observe the student using self-monitoring or when she refrains from overreacting in a tense situation, reinforce her in some meaningful way. Reinforcement might be a sly wink or a smile that communicates that the two of you share a special secret.

31. LOW SELF-ESTEEM

DETECTION Watch for these behaviors.

- Student makes self-depreciating statements
- Student's goals may be unrealistically high
- Student lacks confidence in his abilities
- Student compensates by showing off, boasting, criticizing others
- Student's skills are inadequate
- Student verbalizes in low tones
- Student avoids eye contact
- Student is unaware of his talents

Description. Self-esteem refers to a person's perception of his value or worth as a person. Thus, low self-esteem refers to evaluating oneself as inadequate or inferior. Self-esteem can be interpreted as an aspect of self-concept. In addition to self as knower (intellectual self), self-concept consists of the student's perception of who he is as a physical organism, as a son, as a student, and as a peer (self-identity); of what he wants to be (self-ideal); and of his worth or dignity as a person (self-esteem).

Implications. Everyone experiences feelings of diminished worth from time to time. Such feelings are quite normal as we undergo the ups and downs of life. These feelings are of concern only when they extend over a lengthy period of time and can be associated with general feelings of unhappiness. Intense feelings of low self-esteem and helplessness have been associated with *depression.* When prolonged and serious depression is seen in students, professional assistance must be sought. Self-concept studies show a clear association between positive self-acceptance and healthy adjustment, while negative self-concept is associated with maladjustment. What is associated with low self-esteem in one person may not be in another. For example, one student may be devastated by a fat body and frail performance in sports, while the self-esteem of another student, equally obese and unathletic, remains unaffected by these concerns.

Controlling Factors. Very generally, positive self-esteem is a result of interacting with one's environment in ways that lead to positive reinforcement. Though the process is quite complex, it can be illustrated with an anecdote about a four-year-old girl's introduction to tennis. Andrea was given a suitable racquet and stood on the opposite side of the net as her father threw tennis balls to her forehand side. Andrea missed the first several balls, despite her father's efforts at taking careful aim. She grazed the next ball, only to miss the next two. She hit the next ball over a fence to her left, but missed the ball completely on several subsequent attempts. After hitting three balls in succession (they sailed past her father standing at the net), she jumped with excitement and exclaimed, "Daddy, I'm getting happy!" Good feelings about oneself come from undergoing many such experiences in life, experiences that generate pleasant thoughts and feelings about oneself.

More specifically, self-esteem is largely learned from our successes in mastering early developmental tasks (walking, talking, and so on), from how well we develop academic skills and personal competencies, and especially from our interactions with the important people in our lives (parents, friends, teachers). If, for example, a student's parents devalue his physical characteristics, interests, and competencies, low self-esteem is almost sure to follow. The child who thinks of himself as inferior to others or unworthy because he falls below parental expectations will require many reinforcing experiences before he learns to think of himself in positive ways. Even small difficulties or failures may confirm his sense of inadequacy. On the other hand, the student whose experiences have led to feelings of security and adequacy can adjust to considerable failure without suffering a loss of self-esteem. As children get older, peers and the development of knowledge and skills become increasingly more important in determining their sense of worth. Before turning to suggestions for strengthening self-esteem, two points must be made:

1. Some writers assume that low self-esteem leads to poor academic performance in some children. But the relationship is not clear. In fact, the essential sequence may be quite opposite: Failure in school (or in other areas of life) leads to low self-esteem.
2. Publicly made self-depreciating statements ("I'm so dumb!") may be maintained by the attention and reassurances that follow them ("You're not stupid!"). Positive reinforcement is operating in such cases. In addition, if making negative statements enables the student to avoid tasks ("I can't do it"), he may resort to making similar statements in the future. Negative reinforcement is at work in these cases.

CORRECTION Strategies for altering self-esteem focus on providing students with much more success than failure and on making positive rather than negative self-statements.

1. *Private Talk.* Talk with the student about what he and others expect from his performance. Are these expectations realistic in terms of the student's age and abilities? If the student engages in self-depreciating statements ("I'm dumb," "I can't do anything right"), call this to his attention. Let him know that you are concerned about such statements because he may come to believe that they are true. Try to determine specific areas in which the student feels inadequate: Falling short of parental expectations, not making the baseball team, difficulty in mathematics, and so on. Your basic task is to find ways that will help the student gain success in one or more of these areas. If you think a self-report questionnaire might help identify problem areas, ask your school counselor or psychologist to recommend an appropriate self-concept inventory or school-problem checklist.
2. *Academic Performance.* Do all you can to help the student succeed academically. Learning appropriate skills and becoming knowledgeable about the world will increase the student's chances of interacting successfully with that world. Provide objective information (graphs, charts) relative to the student's progress in math, spelling, and so on.
3. *Schedule Success Conferences.* Meet with the student on a regular basis to acknowledge his recent successes.
4. *Ask for Advice.* Ask the student to advise you in areas in which he feels comfortable. For example, he may be able to help you plan a fieldtrip, organize free-time activities, and so on.
5. *Reward Positive Self-Statements.* Earlier we suggested that teachers "catch students being good." Now we suggest that you teach the student to "catch himself being good." When the student does something well (assisting a classmate), suggest that he compliment himself ("That was a good deed I did"). Praise the student for following your suggestions. You may have to monitor his actions very closely at first, suggesting some appropriate self-compliments. You may also find it necessary to implement a DRO strategy and provide appropriate reinforcement for the absence of negative self-statements. As a variation, ask the student to write positive self-descriptions from time to time. Read each paper and add supportive statements at strategic places ("I agree," "You surely are good in math," "I didn't know you were such an animal lover").
6. *Enlist Parental Support.* The student's sense of worth is not likely to improve if important people in his life are counteracting your efforts at school. Contact your school counselor or local mental health agency. They can suggest teaching materials and appropriate procedures that provide assistance to parents who wish to respond to their child in more positive ways.

7. *Help Establish Friendships.* If appropriate, help the student establish new friendships. Friends who provide positive rather than critical feedback can do wonders for a shaky self-image.
8. *Establish a Buddy System.* Ask the student to join another student in assigned activities extending over several days. For instance, both students could be asked to help in the library, collect tickets at a basketball game, run errands, and so on. Tasks requiring cooperative effort are especially appropriate.
9. *Peer Tutoring.* Allow the student to tutor others. Tutoring younger students may be especially beneficial. Provide plenty of recognition for his efforts.
10. *Discourage Negative Private Dialogues.* Students with a poor self-image may engage in negative thoughts that elicit negative emotional reactions. For example, when meeting someone new, the student might think "He won't like me," or when confronted with a task, his private thoughts might include statements like "I could never do that." If the student lets you in on his private dialogues and you think it will help, suggest some thoughts that are incompatible with the negative ones. People can actually "think themselves" into a more pleasant mood. For example, rather than "I could never do that," suggest "I'll give it a shot and see what happens."

- *Additional Suggestions.* Many students have special talents just waiting to be discovered. Try to identify an area of unrecognized talent—in athletics, music, art, politics, writing, debate, drama, broadcasting—and suggest ways that might help the student develop his competencies in that area.

32. EXCESSIVE WORRY/NERVOUSNESS

DETECTION Watch for these behaviors.

- Student expresses fears, doubts about coping, unrealistic worries
- Student is tense, restless, jittery
- Student's hands tremble, shake, sweat
- Student is afraid that parent will leave or die
- Student is overdependent on others

Description. Excessive worry, nervousness, anxiety, or apprehension are feelings of uneasiness or concern about one's ability to cope with perceived threats. Sometimes a student can be anxious but not know why. The student who worries excessively may appear to be ill at ease, agitated, or distressed. When anxiety becomes intense, the student may experience breathing difficulties, stomachaches, tense muscles, and headaches.

Implications. The nervous child may have difficulty concentrating on school work and may become listless or overactive. These behaviors result in lowered task completion and academic achievement. Some students may become inflexible and have difficulty seeking alternative solutions to academic or social problems. They may make unusual demands for reassurance and question their own competence.

Controlling Factors. Worry and nervousness are reactions to punishing events in a student's life, regardless of whether she is aware of the eliciting events. When worry and anxiety interfere with normal functioning for an extended period of time, the student should be referred to a counseling psychologist. A first step in coping with excessive worry or nervousness is to identify, when possible, the stressful events in a student's life and to take action to resolve their influence. Varying amounts of stress accompany important changes in one's life (moving to a new school), losses (the death of a parent), and pressures to fulfill expectations (high grades). Undue pressure tends to generate excessive worry about performance and rejection by others. Because pressures (expectations) exist in a wide range of situations, it may elicit generalized ("free-floating") feelings of worry or apprehension in the student.

CORRECTION Try one or more of these procedures.

1. *Check Medical Condition.* Discuss the problem with the school nurse and the student's parents to rule out any need for a medical examination. If no medical problem exists, and anxiety is not severe, conduct an ABC analysis (see Chapter 1) to determine possible sources of apprehension. Devise a plan to reduce or eliminate their influence.

2. *Private Talk.* Talk privately with the student to determine whether undue pressure exists in her home. If so, arrange for a parent conference and try to resolve the issue. Many students have realistic fears of illness, nuclear war, pollution, or being bullied. Confront such fears directly. For example, the student could write letters to public officials expressing concern about pollution, or you may be able to offer specific suggestions for coping with a bully.
3. *Situational Changes.* Determine whether your work requirements or other occurrences in the classroom are causing distress. If, for example, your assignments are a source of stress, alter them in some way.
4. *Teach Relaxation.* Teach the student how to relax. Obtain a relaxation-training audiotape and practice relaxing with the student. One technique involves tensing and then relaxing major muscle groups (face, neck, shoulders, arms), so that they are more deeply relaxed following tensing than before. Some students can learn to relax deeply in a few minutes. Other relaxation techniques make use of modeling, meditation, imagining, and thought stopping.
5. *Self-Talk.* After the student can successfully use relaxation techniques, teach her to use self-instruction similar to that described in Problem 1—Impulsiveness. She could, for example, learn to praise herself for staying calm in a stressful situation.
6. *Gradually Introduce Feared Object.* Help the student reduce her fear by gradually exposing her to a fearful situation at the same time she remains relaxed and feels secure. For example, if a student is afraid of swimming in the school swimming pool, she might first watch others enjoy themselves swimming while she remains fully dressed. When she can do this and remain completely relaxed, she might watch in her swimsuit. When she can remain relaxed under these conditions, she might try dangling her feet in the water while sitting at the shallow end of the pool. She moves on *only* when she can remain completely calm during the previous step in the sequence.
7. *Reinforce Approach Behaviors.* Reward closer and closer approaches to the feared situation or event. Because reinforcement can elicit positive feelings as well as strengthen approach behaviors, this is potentially a very effective procedure. The key is to *gradually* approach fearful situations while providing reinforcement at each step.
8. *Catch the Student Relaxing.* Praise the student when you see her in a relaxed state, such as "Jessie, you're doing a good job at that. I see how relaxed and calm you are."

- *Additional Suggestions.* The student may find encouragement in stories about conquering one's fears or succeeding in the face of great adversity.

33. INADEQUATE GROOMING/PERSONAL HYGIENE

DETECTION Watch for these events.

- Student has offensive body odor
- Student's skin, hair, and clothing are dirty
- Student's personal actions are offensive
- Student's clothing is rumpled or in disarray

Description. Inadequate grooming and personal hygiene describes students who are dirty and unkempt and whose personal behaviors are socially offensive and possibly unhealthy. Such students do not bathe regularly, have offensive body odor, and dress in dirty clothing. Some students may pick their nose and either eat the mucus or deposit it on desks, walls, or other public locations. Nail biting, thumbsucking, and scratching are other behaviors that may fit this general category. Younger students frequently pick at scabs, increasing the possibility of infection.

Implications. The main implications of inadequate grooming and personal hygiene pertain to personal health and to social rejection. Inappropriate practices should be monitored for possible damage to the student's general health. Improper personal hygiene practices often result in social rejection and isolation by peers. Name calling and teasing sometimes accompany the rejection.

Controlling Factors. Inadequate grooming and personal hygiene practices typically are not monitored by the student's family for a variety of reasons, including cultural and financial reasons. The behaviors are typically ignored. Or "poor" grooming and personal hygiene may be considered normal and consequently acceptable within the family.

CORRECTION Try one or more of these procedures.

1. *Contact School Nurse.* Arrange for a conference with the school nurse to plan a cooperative course of action. If, in the opinion of the school nurse, active intervention is necessary, determine if the nurse, the teacher, or possibly a social worker needs to be involved. A home visit with the parents might reveal that a social-work approach for the entire family is necessary. Sometimes the school nurse can handle many minor infractions that deal with grooming and personal health. Often such behaviors exist because the student simply has not been taught the proper behaviors.
2. *Private Talk.* Personal grooming and hygiene are private and personal matters. Therefore, your discussion must be conducted in a very sensitive and supportive manner. Many times the student is not aware that his condition or behavior is offensive to others. If financial limitations contribute to the condition, arrange for financial assistance through a social worker and the school principal. The goal of your private talk is to help the student see the need for change and to establish a commitment to change.
3. *Increase Appropriate Information.* Depending on the student's age, obtain from the school librarian or school nurse appropriate books that pertain to the problem. Arrange for the student to read or listen to you read them in private and discuss them with you. Reward the student for his interest in improving his condition, for listening, or for reading the books.
4. *Contracting.* Construct a contract listing specific behaviors to be changed. Consult Chapter 4 for help in writing this contract. In general, you will be providing rewards for appropriate behaviors (hair combed, teeth brushed, shirt buttoned, hands and face washed, shoes polished, and so on). You might also include rewards for the absence of certain behaviors (scab picking, thumbsucking). A contract is more likely to work, of course, if you can enlist the cooperation of the child's parents.

- *Additional Suggestions.* If your curriculum plan provides incentives for reading library books, consider increasing the amount of incentives for reading about grooming and personal hygiene.

34. SOILING/WETTING PANTS

DETECTION Watch for these events.

- Student smells of feces or urine
- Offensive odors are reported by other students
- Clothing gives visible signs of being soiled or wet

Description. Soiling and wetting pants means that the student has had a bowel movement or has urinated while wearing clothing. These "accidents" are mostly seen in preschool and early elementary grades.

Implications. The major implication is social rejection or isolation. However, repeated "accidents" may signal a health problem.

Controlling Factors. Usually, there is no physiological or neurological basis for these events. But persistent problems of soiling and wetting should be referred to the school nurse or a physician before assuming this. When no physiological problem is indicated, soiling and wetting may be due to one or more of the following:

(1) The student may not discriminate the place and time to relieve herself. (Some children may even find it embarrassing to ask.)
(2) Attention following "accidents" may serve to maintain them.
(3) Young children get so caught up in activities that they ignore or fail to discern physical signals until it is too late.

CORRECTION Try one or more of the following procedures.

1. *Preliminary Concerns.* Try to determine whether the student can tell when she needs to use the bathroom. (This information will be helpful in selecting an intervention strategy.) Prior to implementing any plan, record when (time of day), where, and how often "accidents" occur. Ask the parents to send a change of clothes to school each day. Consider requiring replacement clothing that the student dislikes (do not be extreme). If the student lacks prerequisite skills for using the bathroom, a shaping procedure should be implemented. See Chapter 4 for a brief description of this process. You might want to consult the Foxx and Azrin (1973) reference at the end of Part II for a systematic treatment.
2. *Toilet Permission.* Tell the student that she can feel free to go to the toilet anytime that it is necessary. Also explain that it is not necessary to obtain permission from you to do so. You might work out a simple signal that the student can use to let you know when she leaves the room. For example, she might place a book face down on her desk.
3. *Toilet Scheduling.* If the student is unable to go to the toilet under the conditions of Procedure 2, send or take her to the restroom on a regular basis, such as every half hour or every hour. If the student is most likely to soil herself during afternoon hours, send her more often then. If no soiling occurs from one trip to another, provide an appropriate reward (DRO). If soiling does occur, require the student to clean herself and change her clothing. Withhold all reinforcement.
4. *Provide Social Reinforcement.* A few students may soil or wet pants because they receive little positive attention otherwise. If you think this may be the case, find ways to increase the amount of attention the student receives. The student is still required to clean herself and change clothing after each soiling episode.
5. *Response Cost.* Review the section on response cost discussed in Chapter 4. When soiling or wetting occurs, the student must forfeit a reward (points, free time, a privilege). The student is also to clean herself and change clothing.
6. *Time Out.* For every incident of soiling or wetting, require the student to clean herself and change clothing. Then place the student in time out. See the procedures for time out in Chapter 4.
7. *Overcorrection.* If the above procedures fail to work, require the student to clean herself and repeatedly wash her soiled clothing. Make sure this task is not reinforcing in any way. The intensity of this procedure might be increased by also requiring the student to wash other things such as floors, sinks, and so on.

- *Additional Suggestions.* Consider adding positive practice to Procedure 7 above. One possibility requires the student to practice going back and forth to the bathroom as a potential preventative measure against "accidents."

INTRODUCTION

The format of this chapter departs from previous chapters in Part II, since its purpose is to alert you to problem behaviors often associated with special groups of students. First, we discuss some problems with students in special groups who are not handicapped. Then definitions, selected problems, and behavior change strategies are listed for groups of mildly handicapped students.

It is important to remember that when students are viewed as members of special groups, there is no set of social and emotional behaviors that can be attributed to all individuals within that group simply because of their membership in the group. In fact, students assigned to special groups are normal in many respects. Nevertheless, some behaviors *are* correlated with membership in special groups. It is important to note that these correlated behaviors may also be seen in students not assigned to special groups.

Two major instructional concerns—mild behavior problems and underachievement (i.e., achievement below valid expectation)—seem to be paramount when teaching students of special groups (nonhandicapped as well as handicapped). These concerns can best be addressed by using good teaching practices. Good teaching practices involve the consistent application of the principles of behavior discussed in this text to both social and academic performance.

The application of behavioral principles to *social behaviors* (i.e., hitting and fighting) has been discussed in previous chapters and will not be addressed again here. However, intervention strategies related to the instructional problems discussed in this chapter are listed in Table 14-1. The problems themselves were selected from those found in Chapters 6 through 13 and were placed within each category simply by logical analysis. Any given problem might also be logically placed in other categories.

The application of behavioral principles to *academic performance* is reflected in the section on effective instruction sketched in Chapter 4 (pp. 32–33). When you have students with special academic needs, it would be wise to review these pages, paying particular attention to the following two critical elements.

One of the critical elements of effective academic instruction is matching curriculum tasks with the student's level of attained skills ("c" in the sequence listed on page 32). In other words, it is vital that you do not ask the student to perform tasks requiring skills not yet mastered. In the normal hustle and bustle of classroom teaching, this important element of effective instruction is easy to overlook. Its importance cannot be overemphasized because of two research findings: (1) Significant increases in student achievement are observed when curriculum tasks are presented at a level where all prerequisite skills necessary to perform the task have been mastered, and (2) behavior problems are likely to diminish or disappear when students can perform the curriculum tasks presented to them. Three important interpretations can clearly be drawn from these findings: (a) The interaction of behavior problems and academic success must be seriously addressed, (b) it may not be necessary to attack behavior problems prior to expecting good achievement, and (c) academic success breeds good behavior.

Many students are persistently presented with tasks far beyond their current level of skills and ability. Such educational situations are extremely unpleasant for students and can be viewed as punishing. When continually faced with this situation, students react by escaping or avoiding the unrealistic demands. Possible escape and avoidance behaviors include aggressive acts (swearing, destructiveness, scapegoating) and passive or withdrawal reactions (low motivation, inattentiveness, daydreaming). Some students may learn to hate school, experience lower self-esteem, or drop out of school.

The other critical element in effective instruction is flexibility—flexibility in presenting curriculum tasks and in recognizing a variety of student responses ("f" in the sequence listed on page 32). When teaching special groups of students, one realizes that marked individual differences among students are the rule rather than the exception. In order to meet the demands posed by widely disparate individual characteristics, it is important for teachers to depart from group presentations from time to time and to use a variety of auditory and visual presentations during instruction. Accepting a variety of responses with frequent feedback often facilitates learning for some students. For instance, allowing students to choose among response options—such as writing a story, telling or recording a story, doing a special project, or working with a peer—may enable a student to display knowledge and skills that might not have been revealed had one response mode been emphasized.

In sum, good teaching is required to meet the problems faced by students in special groups. Careful sequencing of antecedent materials and events and the arrangement of reinforcing consequences are essential for effective teaching and fruitful learning. *Good teaching is the consistent application of basic behavioral principles to both social and academic performance.*

35. NONHANDICAPPED GROUPS

STUDENTS WITH SITUATIONAL PROBLEMS

Situational problems are transient, temporary concerns of students that affect classroom behavior and achievement. These problems contribute significantly to the stress and strife in the student's life. Often these concerns are not known to the classroom teacher, who may only have noticed a marked change in the student's behavior. When such a change is noticed, the best bet is to use a friendly approach during private talk with the student. Information from the parents, principal, or other professionals might shed light on the situation.

Experienced teachers have seen students whose performance has suffered because of a situational change in their life. For younger students, separating from home or a family member can be quite troublesome. Enrolling in a new school can also cause temporary adjustment problems for some students. Many students find the separation or divorce of their parents especially upsetting. Severe illness of the student or a family member, a recent death of a loved one or friend, or concerns about one's own health and safety all serve as sources of stress for many students.

Student responses to situational problems are as unique as the students. When selecting appropriate interventions, consider those listed for the problems discussed in Chapter 12, "Sense of Self" Problems 29—Daydreaming, 30—Hypersensitivity, 31—Low Self-Esteem, and 32—Excessive Worry/Nervousness. In addition, you might consider the interventions for problems related to verbal behavior (11—Arguing and 13—Swearing/Name Calling), to aggression (14—Destructiveness and 15—Hitting and Fighting), and to social interactions (22—Social Isolation). When the situational problems interfere with academic performance, consult the problem areas in Chapter 6, "Performing School and Academic Tasks."

STUDENTS WHO ARE CULTURALLY DIFFERENT

Students whose cultural background differs from that of other students may present problems for the teacher in both social and academic areas. Some culturally different students are deprived of the economic benefits most students enjoy; others are not. The language usage of some culturally different students departs from that normally used in the classroom.

Teachers seriously uninformed about cultures other than their own may have difficulty identifying appropriate reward and punishment strategies. When rewards for culturally different students are different or in conflict with those of the teacher, the teacher may be at a loss to explain why the student acts as he does. The student's behavior may be interpreted by the teacher as maladaptive when, in fact, it is appropriate for the student's culture. Some cultures might regard questioning the teacher as an insult to the teacher, while the teacher might view the student who does not ask questions as unmotivated or shy. Another student might be assertive and physically aggressive because his culture deems such behavior appropriate if one is to get ahead. But his teacher might view his behavior as rude and disruptive.

While it is important to respect cultural diversity, it is equally important to assist these students to adapt to the mainstream culture, at least during the school day. It is crucial, then, for teachers to learn about the student's cultural values and lifestyle prior to implementing any systematic behavior change plan. Friendly parent conferences and even home visits can be a good source of information. The following chapters may have relevance for some culturally different students: Chapter 6 ("Performing School and Academic Tasks"), Chapter 7 ("Verbal Behavior"), Chapter 8 ("Aggression"), Chapter 9 ("Dishonesty"), and Chapter 10 ("Social Interaction").

STUDENTS WHO ARE GIFTED

Gifted students give evidence of superior performance in intellectual, creative, and/or specific academic areas; in leadership ability; or in the performing and visual arts. These students, in the top 2% of the school population, frequently show an insatiable curiosity, easily grasp concepts, learn independently, and typically enjoy school. However, since some gifted students are underachieving, bored, and do not complete assignments, it is important to maintain an academic challenge. This does not mean doubling homework requirements; it means offering new directions for studying a topic.

Gifted students tend to be socially advanced for their age. Many are natural leaders and organizers, possibly because of their excellent communication skills and attractiveness. However, some gifted students do exhibit behavior problems. They may appear bossy, critical, and overly assertive or too interested in their own ideas to listen to others. Sometimes they feel pressured by high expectations. The following chapters may have relevance for some gifted students: Chapter 7 ("Verbal Behavior") and Chapter 10 ("Social Interaction"). Problems in Chapter 6 ("Performing School and Academic Tasks") might be appropriate for those who are underachieving and unmotivated.

36. HANDICAPPED GROUPS

With the advent of the Education for All Handicapped Children Act, Public Law 94-142 (PL 94-142), in 1975 and its subsequent revisions, most teachers are providing instruction to handicapped students who are placed into regular classes for all or part of the school day. PL 94-142 requires that all exceptional students (i.e., handicapped students who require special education and related services) must receive a free and appropriate education.

An Individualized Education Program (IEP)—a written document specifying long range goals and short term instructional objectives appropriate to the individual—must be prepared for each student. The handicapped student's education must be provided in a Least Restrictive Environment (LRE), one in which the student is educated to the maximum extent appropriate with non-handicapped students. For most mildly handicapped students, this environment is the regular classroom. Placing handicapped students in the regular classroom is termed *mainstreaming.*

Even though mainstreamed students and their regular classroom teachers are to receive the services of special education consultants or resource room teachers, the placement of handicapped students in the regular classroom has caused many of these educators to be concerned about their skills in offering an appropriate education for handicapped students. Their concern is usually focused on behavior problems and academic achievement. These are the same concerns faced by teachers of special groups of nonhandicapped students, discussed in the introduction to this chapter. We now turn to a brief discussion of cross-categorical and traditional handicapped students.

CROSS-CATEGORICAL HANDICAPPED STUDENTS

Traditionally, handicapped students have been categorized according to cognitive, sensory, or physical/health handicap and the degree of handicap. But recently, some educators have proposed that the learning needs of handicapped students are similar across some categories. They have put forth the notion of *cross-categorical* (i.e., *generic, noncategorical*) groups, wherein students of different traditional groupings are placed together in a new classification based on the severity of the handicap or on educational needs. For example, the grouping termed Educationally Handicapped might include students traditionally labeled mildly mentally handicapped, emotionally disturbed, or learning disabled. Other groupings might combine students according to degree of handicap, such as mild/moderate and severe/profound. Some sections of the county may have classification systems different from others. For instance, some programs may combine two categories into one (Orthopedic/Health Impaired) while others may not specify the handicap (the student must "meet the criteria"). Others may define special groups by common characteristics ("short attention span").

Regardless of how handicapped students are grouped, they often present behavior management and underachievement problems. Intervention procedures in Chapter 6 ("Performing School and Academic Tasks") seem particularly appropriate for underachieving students. For handicapping conditions correlated with developmental delays, consider the problems in Chapter 11 ("Immaturity"), especially 27—Overactivity.

For handicapped students displaying frequent maladaptive behavior, the discussion of problems in Chapter 8 ("Aggression") and Chapter 7 ("Verbal Behavior") may be appropriate. For mainstreamed students who find social interaction with nonhandicapped peers troublesome, the explanation of problems in Chapter 10 ("Social Interaction") and Chapter 12 ("Sense of Self") may offer useful interventions. Problems in Chapter 13 ("The Body and Personal Habits") may be relevant for seriously impaired students. Students with moderate to severe cognitive handicaps might also benefit from the interventions described in Chapter 9 ("Dishonesty"), since those students may not be fully aware of the meaning and consequences of their behavior.

TRADITIONAL CATEGORIES OF HANDICAPPED STUDENTS

Traditional categories and definitions based on federal law (PL 94–142) and related problems for each are given in Table 14-1 on pages 150-151. Categories and definitions in some states and local school districts may differ from those on this list. The behaviors listed were selected as likely correlates with each category and are listed alphabetically. The number beside each problem directs you to the discussion of that problem in the text. These problems are not necessarily representative of the categories or exclusive to them. Obviously, all behaviors would not apply to any one student within a category.

CLOSING COMMENT

The most fundamental purpose of educators is to improve the quality of life of *all* students. The techniques in this book are designed to enable you to accomplish this goal. By effecting positive change in student behavior in a deliberate and systematic way, you improve the lives of the students as well as enrich the lives of those who teach them.

TABLE 14-1 Traditional Categories, Definitions, and Related Behaviors of Handicapped Students

Category	PL 94-142 Definitions	Related Behaviors
Emotionally Disturbed/ Behavior Disordered	Over a long period of time and to a marked degree, these conditions adversely affect educational performance: inability to learn not explained by sensory, intellectual, or health factors; inability to build/ maintain satisfactory interpersonal relations with peers or teachers; inappropriate behaviors or feelings under normal circumstances; general pervasive mood of unhappiness or depression; tendency to develop physical symptoms or fears associated with personal or school problems. Autistic children are not included in this definition.	Annoying Others—19 Arguing—11 Attention-Seeking—23 Daydreaming—29 Destructiveness—14 Excessive Worry/Nervousness—32 Hitting and Fighting—15 Impulsiveness—1 Interrupting—12 Low Self-Esteem—31 Noncompliance—4 Out-of-Seat—5 Overactivity—27 Social Isolation—22 Swearing/Name Calling—13 Talking without Permission—6 Unmotivated to Learn—7
Specific Learning Disability (SLD)	A disorder in one or more of the basic psychological processes involved in understanding and using language, spoken or written, which may manifest itself in an imperfect ability to listen, think, speak, read, write, spell, or do mathematical calculations. The term includes such conditions as perceptual handicaps, brain injury, minimal brain dysfunction, dyslexia, and developmental aphasia. Not included are learning problems primarily the result of vision, hearing, or motor handicaps; mental retardation; emotional disturbance; or environmental, cultural, or economic disadvantage.	Impulsiveness—1 Inattention—2 Interrupting—12 Low Self-Esteem—31 Noncompletion of Tasks—3 Out-of-Seat—5 Overactivity—27 Overdependence—28 Social Isolation—22 Talking without Permission—6 Unprepared for Class—8 Unsatisfactory Homework—10

TABLE 14-1 (Continued)

Category	PL 94-142 Definitions	Related Behaviors
Mildly Mentally Handicapped	Significant subaverage general intellectual functioning existing concurrently with deficits in adaptive behavior and manifested during the developmental period, that adversely affects a child's educational performance.	Inattention—2 Inadequate Grooming/Personal Hygiene—33 Low Self-Esteem—31 Overactivity—27 Overdependence—28 Scapegoat—20 Social Isolation—22 Unmotivated to Learn—7 Unprepared for Class—8 Unsatisfactory Homework—10
Communication Disordered	Stuttering, impaired articulation, a language impairment, or a voice impairment, that adversely affects a child's educational performance.	Destructiveness—14 Excessive Worry/Nervousness—32 Hitting and Fighting—15 Inattention—2 Low Self-Esteem—31 Scapegoat—20 Shyness/Withdrawal—21 Social Isolation—22 Unmotivated to Learn—7
Visually Impaired	A visual impairment that, even with correction, adversely affects a child's educational performance. The term includes both partially seeing and blind children.	Low Self Esteem—31 Overdependence—28 Shyness/Withdrawal—21 Social Isolation—22 Unmotivated to Learn—7
Hearing Impaired	Fluctuating or permanent impairment that adversely affects a child's educational performance. The child is not deaf.	Daydreaming—29 Hitting and Fighting—15 Shyness/Withdrawal—21 Social Isolation—22 Unmotivated to Learn—7
Physically Handicapped/ Health Impaired	Orthopedic impairment adversely affects educational performance. It is caused by congenital anomaly, disease, or other causes. "Health-impaired" concerns limited strength, vitality, or alertness.	Arguing—11 Inadequate Grooming/Personal Hygiene—33 Noncompletion of Tasks—3 Overdependence—28 Shyness/Withdrawal—21 Social Isolation—22 Soiling/Wetting Pants—34 Swearing/Name Calling—13 Unmotivated to Learn—7

REFLECTIONS

1. Part II placed problems of concern to teachers of regular, remedial, and special education students into eight categories (chapters). Compare the problems in two or more categories. Are there distinct differences in the behaviors or do some behaviors fit more than one category? How are the implications of the problems similar? How are they different? How divergent are the controlling factors?
2. Labels given to behaviors mean different things to different people. Consider some of the words used in Part II to label problem behaviors. Do you think other labels would be more appropriate? For example, is *anxiety* (or *apprehension* or *nervousness*) a better label than *excessive worry?* Is the term *self-concept* (or *ego strength*) more appropriate than *self-esteem?* Why or why not?
3. Several recommendations for reducing impulsiveness are presented in Chapter 6. Make one list of recommendations that involve reducing impulsiveness and one for recommendations that involve increasing other performance. Is there a greater emphasis on reducing or increasing behavior? Does this emphasis hold across other problem areas?
4. Many procedures for changing behavior are available to teachers. Interview an experienced special education teacher to determine his or her perception of effective procedures to use with one or more of the problems listed in Part II. Compare the teacher's recommendations with those presented in this book.
5. Because of intermittent reinforcement, some behaviors become habits and are quite difficult to change. Based on your experiences, which of the behaviors presented in Part II are generally most difficult to change? Which of these would probably require the most teacher attention or classroom restructuring?
6. Some teachers have said that lack of motivation, talking and leaving one's seat without permission, coming to class unprepared, and noncompliance are the most persistent problems facing classroom teachers. Given your experiences in education, do you agree with this list? How would you change it?
7. Personal interaction with many students allows us to observe a wide variety of behaviors. Based on your contact with handicapped children and nonhandicapped children, return to Chapter 14 and add problem behaviors you think are missing in each of the categories listed in Table 14-1. Then speculate about which behaviors are most correlated with each condition or category.
8. Select one of your students, one you know well, or obtain a case study of a student. On the left side of a sheet of paper, outline the nine-step plan introduced in Chapter 1. On the right side, sketch a plausible behavior change plan using the intervention strategies presented in Chapter 4 and in Part II. Discuss your efforts with someone in your field.

9. Many textbooks, workbooks, and manuals offer procedures for changing the behavior of students. Select several problem behaviors and read the advice given for these behaviors in one or more of the references at the end of this section. Add the references you like to the appropriate sections in this text for future reference.
10. The National Education Association (NEA), the Council for Exceptional Children (CEC), and the American Association of School Administrators (AASA) have published an official statement strongly supporting continued cooperation between general educators and special educators to improve the education of all exceptional children and youth and children and youth in general. Interview a special education teacher, a regular education teacher, and a school administrator to solicit their reactions to this commitment to cooperate. To what extent do they agree? How do they disagree? What specific actions support their viewpoints? What actions belie their positions?
11. Public Law 94-142 mandates that exceptional children and youth be educated in the least restrictive environment to the maximum extent possible, as long as that environment is appropriate for the student's individual education program. Interview a school principal and determine how many handicapped students are mainstreamed into each classroom and grade at her school. Discuss the behaviors of mainstreamed students that present the most problems from the principal's viewpoint. How do these behaviors compare with those presented in Chapter 14?
12. The Council for Exceptional Children (CEC) is the professional organization that serves as an advocate for all exceptional children. Ask the director of special education in a local school system when the statewide meeting of CEC is held in your state. Make arrangements to attend the conference. Participate in the sessions that concern the types of behavior demonstrated by students in your classroom. Write a brief report of how you will use what you learned from the conference and how it compares with the behaviors cited in Chapter 14.
13. While no given set of behaviors belongs exclusively to any category of students, certain behaviors do seem to be correlated with certain categories of students. Based on the different categories of students identified in Chapter 14, which type of handicapped student would you be most comfortable teaching? Which type would you be hesitant to have in your classroom? Why?
14. Arrange for an interview with a special education teacher or with the director of special education in a local school system. Discuss the characteristics and instructional strategies that would be appropriate for the type of handicapped student you would hesitate to teach. Ask permission to visit a classroom with students having that particular handicapping condition. Ask the teacher about the joys and frustrations with students in her classroom. After your visit, write a brief summary of your reactions. Has your attitude toward students with the handicap changed? Why?

15. Volunteer to assist a teacher with some mainstreamed students by observing and recording the baseline for one or more students. You and the teacher must first agree on a clear description of the target behavior (write it down). Select the appropriate recording technique to use with the target behavior. After data are collected, put them on a chart or graph. Discuss with the teacher the events that were antecedent and consequent to the target behavior. Determine what rewards he might try in a behavior change plan. If time permits, continue to observe and record the target behavior throughout the behavior change plan.
16. Find a recent text or journal that covers behavior problems and/or major topics in the field of special education. Compare your reading with the content of Part II. The names of some references are listed here and on the next page.

Ayllon, T., & McKittrick, S. M. (1982). *How to set up a token economy.* Austin, TX: Pro-ed.

Azrin, N. H., & Besalel, V. A. (1980). *How to use overcorrection.* Lawrence, KS: H & H Enterprises, Inc.

Baer, D. M. (1981). *How to plan for generalization.* Lawrence, KS: H & H Enterprises, Inc.

Blackham, G. J., & Silberman, A. (1980). *Modification of child and adolescent behavior.* Belmont, CA: Wadsworth.

Esveldt-Dawson, K., & Kazdin, A. E. (1982). *How to use self-control.* Austin, TX: Pro-ed.

Foxx, R. M., & Azrin, N. H. (1973). *Dry pants: A rapid method of toilet training children. Behavior Research and Therapy, 11,* 435–442.

Hall, R. V., & Hall, M. C. (1980). *How to use systematic attention and approval (social reinforcement).* Austin, TX: Pro-ed.

Hall, R. V., & Hall, M. C. (1980). *How to use time out.* Lawrence, KS: H & H Enterprises, Inc.

Hall, R. V., & Hall, M. C. (1982). *How to negotiate a behavioral contract.* Lawrence, KS: H & H Enterprises, Inc.

Hallahan, D. P., & Kauffman, J. M. (1988). *Exceptional children: Introduction to special education* (4th ed.). Englewood Cliffs, NJ: Prentice-Hall.

Houten, R. V. (1980). *How to motivate others through feedback.* Austin, TX: Pro-ed.

Houten, R. V. (1980). *How to use reprimands.* Lawrence, KS: H & H Enterprises, Inc.

Index

E

F

G

H

I

R

S

T

ABOUT THE AUTHORS

FRANK J. SPARZO holds a Ph.D. from the Johns Hopkins University and is presently on the Graduate Faculty and Professor of Psychology in Educational Psychology at Ball State University. During 1987-88, he was Visiting Professor in Educational Studies at the University of Delaware. He serves on the editorial boards of professional journals, has published articles on the effect of testing formats on academic performance, and has served as a behavioral consultant for a number of public schools. Author of a Phi Delta Kappa Fastback on behavior change, he has lectured and conducted workshops on behavior change for teachers and professional groups in many states throughout the nation.

JAMES A. POTEET holds a Ph.D. in Special Education from Purdue University and is presently on the Graduate Faculty and Professor of Special Education at Ball State University. He co-edited a monograph on special education assessment for the Council for Educational Diagnostic Services (CEDS), a division of Council for Exceptional Children (CEC). He currently serves as Governor of CEDS and has served as its president. He has published articles on assessment practices, conducted workshops, and served on the editorial board of a number of professional journals. He is also the co-author of *Assessing and Programming Basic Curriculum Skills* (Allyn and Bacon, 1987), and author of texts on behavior modification and educational evaluation in special education.

READER'S REACTION

Dear Reader:

No one knows better than you the special needs of your students or the exact nature of your classroom problems. Your analysis of the extent to which this book meets *your* special needs will help us revise and improve this book, and assist us in developing other books in the *Allyn and Bacon Detecting and Correcting Series.*

Please take a few minutes to respond to the questionnaire on the next page. If you would like to receive a reply to your comments or additional information about the series, indicate this preference in your answer to the last question. Mail the completed form to:

Joyce S. Choate, Consulting Editor
Detecting and Correcting Series
c/o Allyn and Bacon, Inc.
160 Gould Street
Needham Heights, Massachusetts 02194-2310

Thank you for sharing your special needs and professional concerns.

Sincerely,

Joyce S. Choate

Joyce S. Choate

READER'S REACTION TO

Classroom Behavior: Detecting and Correcting Special Problems

Name: ____________ Position: ____________

Address: ____________ ____________

____________ Date: ____________

1. How have you used this book?

   ___College Text ___Inservice Training ___Teaching Resource

Describe:____

2. For which purpose(s) do you recommend its use?

3. What do you view as the major strengths of the book?

4. What are its major weaknesses?

5. How could the book be improved?

6. What additional topics should be included in this book?

7. In addition to the books currently included in the *Allyn and Bacon Detecting and Correcting Series*—Basic Mathematics, Classroom Behavior, Language Arts, and Reading—what other books would you recommend developing?

8. Would you like to receive these items?

   ___A reply to your comments

   ___Additional information about this series

Additional Comments:

THANK YOU FOR SHARING YOUR SPECIAL NEEDS AND PROFESSIONAL CONCERNS